Multifamily HomePlans

115 Duplex, Multiplex & Townhome Designs

HOME PLANNERS

Published by Home Planners, LLC

Wholly owned by Hanley-Wood, LLC

3275 West Ina Road, Suite 110

Tucson, Arizona 85741

Distribution Center:

29333 Lorie Lane

Wixom, Michigan 48393

Jayne Fenton, President

Linda B. Bellamy, Executive Editor

Arlen Feldwick-Jones, Editorial Director

Vicki Frank, Managing Editor

Marian E. Haggard, Editor

Ashleigh Stone, Plans Editor

Jay C. Walsh, Graphic Designer

Teralyn Morriss, Graphic Production Artist

Sara Lisa, Senior Production Manager

Fariba Crawford, Production Manager

©2002 by Home Planners, LLC

First Edition, March 2002

10 9 8 7 6 5 4 3 2

Printed in the United States of America.

Library of Congress Catalog Card Number: 2001099017

ISBN softcover: 1-881955-99-0

Cover House: Designed by Home Design Alternatives, Inc., plan HPT260072 offers many attractive amenities. See page 75 for further information.

Title Page: Plan HPT260061 is designed by Home Design Alternatives, Inc., and may be found on page 64.

Table of Contents

Townhome Plans

This home, as shown in the photograph, may differ from the actual blueprints. For more detailed information, please check the floor plans carefully.

Photo by Jeffrey Jacobs/Mims Studios

Plan HPT260001

Unit A
First Floor: 1,063 sq. ft.
Second Floor: 886 sq. ft.
Total: 1,949 sq. ft.

Unit B
First Floor: 836 sq. ft.
Second Floor: 771 sq. ft.
Total: 1,607 sq. ft.

Unit C
First Floor: 904 sq. ft.
Second Floor: 839 sq. ft.
Total: 1,743 sq. ft.

Width: 22'-6"
Depth: 76'-9"

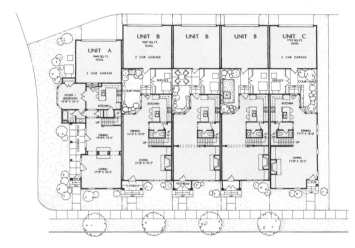

Erin's Isle

Row houses offer unique solutions for narrow-lot spaces and provide a sense of unity. The middle three units provide identical floor plans, with an entry porch or vestibule that opens to a living room with a centerpiece fireplace. The second floor includes a family bedroom with a bath, and a master suite with a balcony. Unit A, a corner home, is enhanced by a covered front porch and balcony and features a through-fireplace shared by the dining and living rooms. A flex room easily converts to a study or bedroom with its own bath. Unit C, also a corner home, provides open views from the open living and dining rooms and, upstairs—a generous master suite.

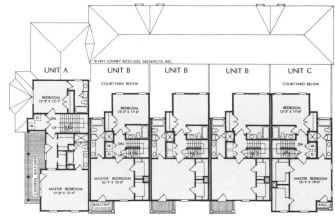

4

Plan HPT260002

Unit A
First Floor: 839 sq. ft.
Second Floor: 787 sq. ft.
Total: 1,626 sq. ft.
Unit B
First Floor: 772 sq. ft.
Second Floor: 768 sq. ft.
Total: 1,540 sq. ft.

Unit C
First Floor: 772 sq. ft.
Second Floor: 784 sq. ft.
Total: 1,556 sq. ft.
Bonus Room: 267 sq. ft.
Unit D
First Floor: 772 sq. ft.
Second Floor: 735 sq. ft.
Total: 1,507 sq. ft.
Bonus Room: 352 sq. ft.

Width: 22'-11"
Depth: 46'-6"

Greenbriar Road

Covered porches provide plenty of opportunities for enjoying the outdoor spaces of these captivating row houses. The corner home, Unit A, offers a walk-through kitchen that leads to the dining area. The second floor includes a master suite with a private deck. Unit B, represented twice in this arrangement, includes a U-shaped kitchen. Upstairs, the master suite boasts a rear deck. Unit C provides a vaulted master suite on the second floor. The open formal rooms of Unit D, a corner home, lead outdoors to a wraparound porch. Upstairs, the master suite enjoys a private deck.

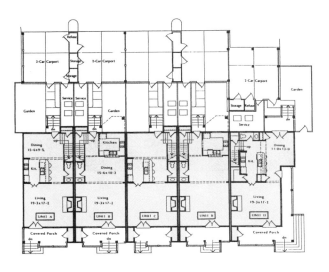

This home, as shown in the photograph, may differ from the actual blueprints. For more detailed information, please check the floor plans carefully.

Photo by Jeffrey Jacobs/Mims Studios

This home, as shown in the photograph, may differ from the actual blueprints.
For more detailed information, please check the floor plans carefully.

Photo by Jeffrey Jacobs/Mims Studios

Plan HPT260003

Unit A & C
First Floor: 970 sq. ft.
Second Floor: 970 sq. ft.
Third Floor: 351 sq. ft
Total: 2,291 sq. ft.
Unit B & D
First Floor: 940 sq. ft.
Second Floor: 940 sq. ft.
Third Floor: 299 sq. ft
Total: 2,179 sq. ft.

Width: 23'-0"
Depth: 42'-0"

Bryce Boulevard

A refined row house, this design is a perfect fit for the center of the neighborhood. With tidy covered entries, a stately facade provides plenty of curb appeal. Each floor plan offers spacious formal rooms, a massive hearth, a casual dining area and a private breezeway and patio. The second floor includes a lavish master suite with a private fireplace, two walk-in closets and access to an upper-level loft with its own bath. The dining room or den of Unit A leads outdoors to a private patio and covered breezeway. Unit B provides a service entrance and a rear staircase that leads to outdoor areas. The garage for each unit is placed to the rear of the property.

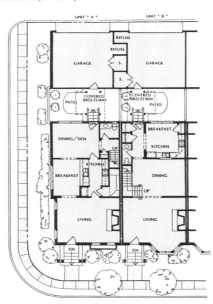

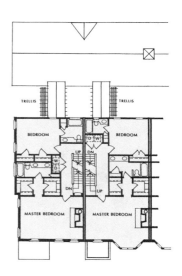

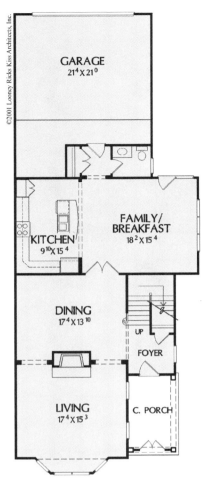

©2001 Looney Ricks Kiss Architects, Inc.

GARAGE
21⁴ X 21⁰

KITCHEN
9¹⁰ X 15⁴

FAMILY/ BREAKFAST
18² X 15⁴

DINING
17⁴ X 13¹⁰

UP

FOYER

LIVING
17⁴ X 15³

C. PORCH

BEDROOM 2
11⁰ X 14⁶

BATH 2

BEDROOM 3
11⁰ X 15³

MSTR. BATH

DN

MASTER BEDROOM
17⁴ X 15³

C. BAL.

Plan HPT260004

First Floor: 1,237 sq. ft.
Second Floor: 1,098 sq. ft.
Total: 2,335 sq. ft.

Width: 29'-4"
Depth: 73'-0"

Marian Meadows

The curb appeal of this home can be found in the dazzling details: a bay window, twin sconces illuminating a columned porch, a pretty portico and classic shutters. The foyer opens to the formal living and dining rooms, subtly defined by a central fireplace. The gourmet kitchen overlooks a spacious family/breakfast area, which leads outdoors. The second floor includes a lavish master suite with a spa-style tub and a private covered balcony. The secondary sleeping area is connected by a gallery hall and a stair landing.

This home, as shown in the photograph, may differ from the actual blueprints. For more detailed information, please check the floor plans carefully.

Photo by Jeffrey Jacobs/Mims Studios

Plan HPT260005

First Floor: 1,282 sq. ft.
Second Floor: 956 sq. ft.
Total: 2,238 sq. ft.

Width: 30'-2"
Depth: 74'-2"

Holroyd Heights

There won't be any chilly mornings for the homeowner within this lovely townhome. The second-floor master suite boasts a massive hearth, flanked by built-in shelves. French doors open from the bedroom to a private balcony, where gentle breezes may invigorate the senses. A gallery hall leads to a secondary bedroom, which offers its own bath and a walk-in closet. On the first floor, formal rooms share a through-fireplace and offer doors to the veranda and garden court. A secluded study easily converts to a guest suite or home office, and convenient storage space is available in the rear-loading garage.

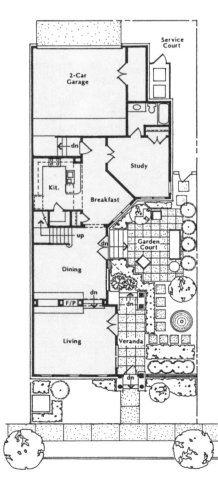

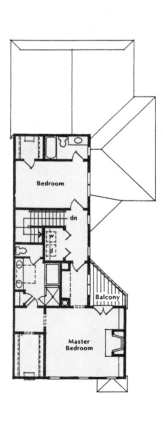

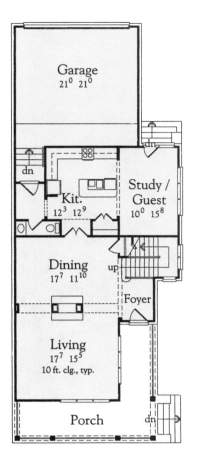

Garage
21⁰ 21⁰

Kit.
12³ 12⁹

Study / Guest
10⁰ 15⁸

Dining
17⁷ 11¹⁰

up

Foyer

Living
17⁷ 15⁵
10 ft. clg., typ.

Porch

dn

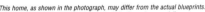

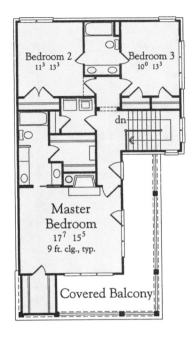

Bedroom 2
11³ 13³

Bedroom 3
10⁰ 13³

dn

Master Bedroom
17⁷ 15⁵
9 ft. clg., typ.

Covered Balcony

Plan HPT260006

First Floor: 1,135 sq. ft.
Second Floor: 1,092 sq. ft.
Total: 2,227 sq. ft.

Width: 28'-8"
Depth: 74'-2"

London Plaza

Stylish square columns line the porch and portico of this townhome, which has received the *Builder's Choice National Design and Planning Award* and the *Award of Merit in Architecture*. Inside, an open arrangement of the formal rooms is partially defined by a through-fireplace. Brightened by a triple window, the breakfast nook is an inviting place for family and friends to gather. A single door opens to the outside, where steps lead down to the rear property—a good place to start a walk into town. The kitchen features a food-prep island and a sizable pantry. Upstairs, the master suite offers a fireplace and access to the portico.

This home, as shown in the photograph, may differ from the actual blueprints. For more detailed information, please check the floor plans carefully.

Photo by Jeffrey Jacobs/Mims Studios

9

This home, as shown in the photograph, may differ from the actual blueprints. For more detailed information, please check the floor plans carefully.

Photo by Jeffrey Jacobs/Mims Studios

Plan HPT260007

First Floor: 952 sq. ft.
Second Floor: 766 sq. ft.
Total: 1,718 sq. ft.

Width: 24'-2"
Depth: 74'-2"

Catherine Commons

This stunning townhouse has a breezy disposition yet, inside, provides the perfect blend of formality and comfort. The plan includes an open dining/living area with a hearth and a bay window. A flex room serves as a study or guest bedroom with private access to a hall bath. The U-shaped kitchen surrounds casual dining space, which overlooks the covered porch. The second floor offers a vaulted master bedroom that leads to both a private and a shared balcony through two sets of lovely French doors.

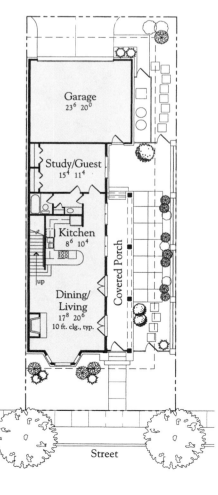

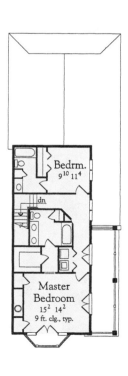

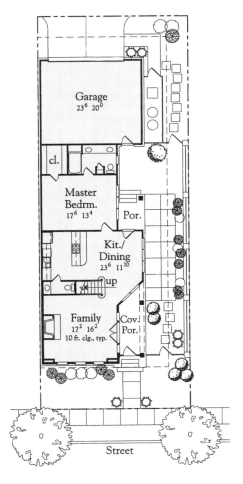

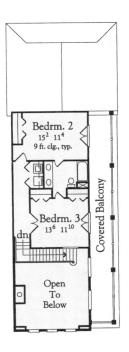

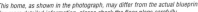

Plan HPT260008

First Floor: 1,075 sq. ft.
Second Floor: 604 sq. ft.
Total: 1,679 sq. ft.

Width: 24'-2"
Depth: 74'-2"

Cluck's Corner

This townhouse variation provides a comfortable interior, tailored for couples and families. The front porch leads to a spacious family room with a fireplace and a three-window view. A galley-style kitchen opens to casual dining space, which offers access to a side porch with steps down to a courtyard. The first-floor master suite provides a walk-in closet and additional linen storage in the bath. Upstairs, each of two family bedrooms provides a set of French doors to the upper porch as well as private access to the shared bath.

This home, as shown in the photograph, may differ from the actual blueprints. For more detailed information, please check the floor plans carefully.

Photo by Jeffrey Jacobs/Mims Studios

Plan HPT260009

First Floor: 781 sq. ft.
Second Floor: 1,034 sq. ft.
Total: 1,815 sq. ft.

Width: 19'-9"
Depth: 69'-0"

This home, as shown in the photograph, may differ from the actual blueprints. For more detailed information, please check the floor plans carefully.

Photo by Jeffrey Jacobs/Mims Studios

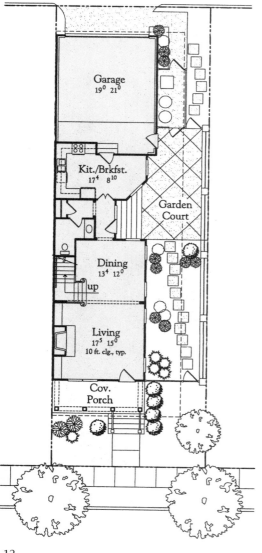

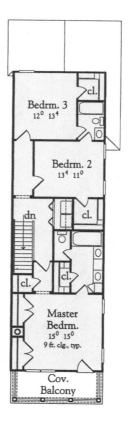

Tompkins Way

Here's a townhome that's both beautiful and compact. The fortunate homeowner will never feel crowded, with a well-drawn interior of spacious rooms and plenty of indoor/outdoor flow. A double portico presents a charming welcome and invites enjoyment of the outdoors. The entry leads to an open arrangement of the living and dining rooms, warmed by a fireplace. A center hall provides access to a garden court and path, where family members can linger or begin their stroll to Main Street shops. Upstairs, the sleeping quarters include two secondary bedrooms and a master suite that opens to a covered balcony.

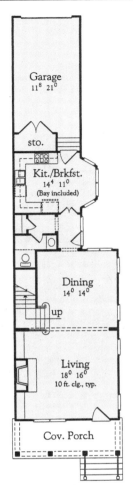

Garage
11⁸ 21⁰

sto.

Kit./Brkfst.
14⁴ 11⁰
(Bay included)

Dining
14⁰ 14⁰

up

Living
18⁰ 16⁰
10 ft. clg., typ.

Cov. Porch

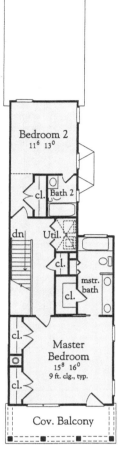

Bedroom 2
11⁶ 13⁰

cl. Bath 2

dn   Util.

cl.

mstr.
bath

cl.

cl.

Master
Bedroom
15⁸ 16⁰
9 ft. clg., typ.

cl.

Cov. Balcony

Plan HPT260010

First Floor: 804 sq. ft.
Second Floor: 835 sq. ft.
Total: 1,639 sq. ft. per unit

Width: 18'-8"
Depth: 80'-6"

Frederick Avenue

This lovely design is much more than just a pretty face. A row of symmetrical exteriors creates a stunning streetscape, but the real beauty is within each home. A well-organized interior arranges the formal rooms to accommodate gatherings both grand and cozy. A centered fireplace lends warmth and a sense of comfort to the living room and shares its glow with the formal dining room. A U-shaped kitchen overlooks a breakfast bay with three windows. Upstairs, the master suite provides a covered balcony and a double-bowl vanity.

This home, as shown in the photograph, may differ from the actual blueprints. For more detailed information, please check the floor plans carefully.

Photo by Jeffrey Jacobs/Mims Studios

Plan HPT260011

First Floor: 684 sq. ft.
Second Floor: 657 sq. ft.
Total: 1,341 sq. ft. per unit
Basement: 166 sq. ft. per unit

Width: 54'-0"
Depth: 46'-0"

Mauleita Way

These timeless townhome designs are dazzled in old-fashioned accents that enclose three comfortable levels of livability. For each unit, a cozy covered front porch is just right for refreshing outdoor relaxation. Enter inside, where a two-sided fireplace warms the family room and breakfast area. The second level offers enough room for a new family with a master bedroom enlarged by a sitting area, a walk-in closet and a private bath. The second bedroom—perfect for a nursery or home office—features a private shower bath. A washer and dryer area is featured on this floor for family convenience. The basement level offers storage space and a garage.

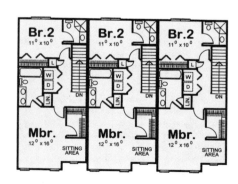

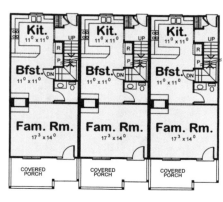

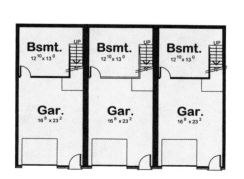

Molly Circle

These simple townhome designs boast efficient space wrapped in a moderate square footage. The first level of each unit is virtually identical, starting with a covered stoop that enters inside to a spacious family room. This room connects to a breakfast room and a compact kitchen located at the rear. A laundry room and powder room are tucked behind the staircase. One option for the second floor provides a master suite with a walk-in closet and private bath, and two additional bedrooms that share a hall bath. Another option provides a master bedroom and secondary bedroom—each with a walk-in closet—and an open space that allows a two-story family room.

Plan HPT260012

Units A & C
First Floor: 1,008 sq. ft.
Second Floor: 921 sq. ft.
Total: 1,929 sq. ft.
Unit B
First Floor: 1,008 sq. ft.
Second Floor: 554 sq. ft.
Total: 1,562 sq. ft. per unit

Width: 72'-0"
Depth: 42'-0"

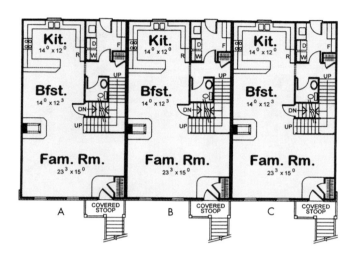

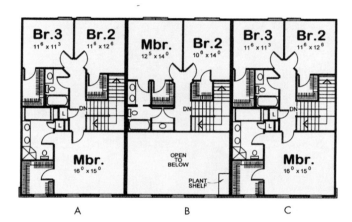

Plan HPT260013

First Floor: 904 sq. ft.
Second Floor: 1,058 sq. ft.
Total: 1,962

Width: 22'-0"
Depth: 74'-0"

Bambrough Bay

Reminiscent of the popular "shotgun" homes of the past, this fine clapboard home is perfect for urban or riverfront living. Two balconies grace the second floor—one at the front and one on the side. A two-way fireplace between the formal living and dining rooms provides visual impact. Built-in bookcases flank an arched opening between these rooms. A pass-through from the kitchen to the dining room simplifies serving, and a walk-in pantry provides storage. On the second floor, the master bedroom opens to a large balcony, and the relaxing master bath is designed with a separate shower and an angled whirlpool tub. Two secondary bedrooms and a full bath are located at the rear of the plan. Please specify crawlspace or slab foundation when ordering.

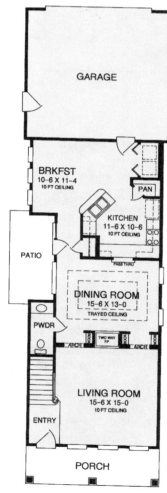

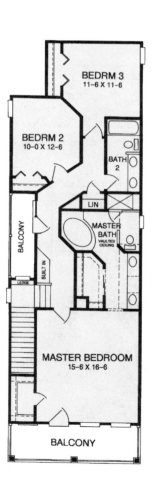

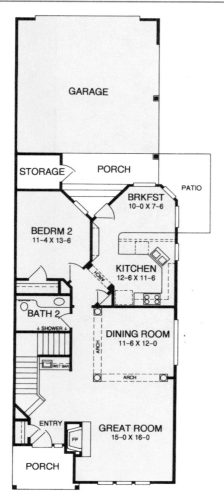

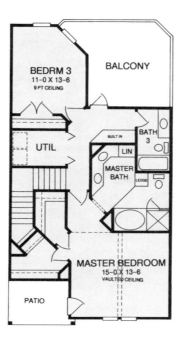

First Floor: 1,078 sq. ft.
Second Floor: 921 sq. ft.
Total: 1,999

Width: 24'-11"
Depth: 73'-10"

The Holley House

This charming clapboard home is loaded with character and is perfect for a narrow lot. Columns and connecting arches separate the great room and the dining room. The efficient U-shaped kitchen features a corner sink with a window view and a bayed breakfast area with access to the rear porch. A bedroom and a bath are conveniently located for guests on the first floor. Upstairs, the master suite features a vaulted ceiling and a luxurious bath with dual vanities, a whirlpool tub and a separate shower. A secondary bedroom and a full bath are also located on the second floor with a large rear balcony completing this highly livable plan. Please specify crawlspace or slab foundation when ordering.

Plan HPT260015

First Floor: 911 sq. ft.
Second Floor: 1,029 sq. ft.
Total: 1,940

Width: 20'-10"
Depth: 75'-10"

Keota Lane

This aesthetically pleasing home offers a well-balanced floor plan that starts with the two front covered porches that make up the facade. Floor-to-ceiling windows brighten the front rooms, which focus on the see-through fireplace at the center. A gourmet kitchen with a pantry and an island looks onto the side patio. Upstairs, a built-in desk allows for study. All bedrooms access one of the porches. A two-car garage lies at the rear of the home and opens to the kitchen.

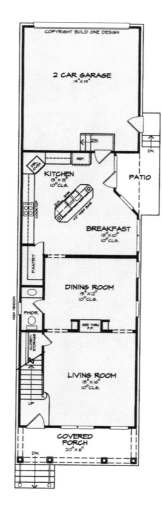

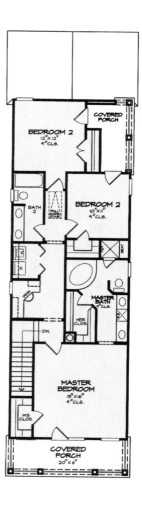

Crown Gardens

Welcome home to gracious living in this stately duplex. The brick facade, accented with shutters and columned porches, is refined and friendly at the same time. The twin plans are laid out with the same simple elegance: the covered porch opens to the spacious family room, which in turn flows right into the kitchen/dining area. A snack-bar counter breaks up this space and also makes a nice spot for casual meals. A roomy pantry and a utility room further enhance the kitchen. A short hallway from the dining area opens to a powder room and to the master bedroom, which is nicely furnished with a deluxe private bath and a huge walk-in closet. Upstairs, two bedrooms, a full bath and two linen closets make for ideal sleeping quarters.

Plan HPT262001

First Floor: 1,077 sq. ft.
Second Floor: 662 sq. ft.
Total: 1,739 sq. ft. per unit

Width: 47'-10"
Depth: 51'-10"

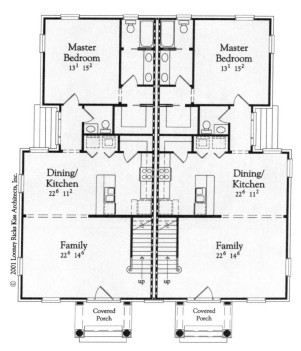

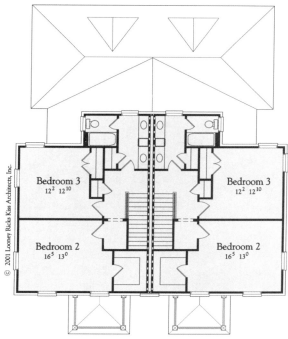

Plan HPT262002

Unit A
First Floor: 1,059 sq. ft.
Second Floor: 633 sq. ft.
Total: 1,692 sq. ft.
Unit B
First Floor: 1,094 sq. ft.
Second Floor: 665 sq. ft.
Total: 1,759 sq. ft.

Width: 47'-10"
Depth: 51'-10"

Venice Chapel

Front and side porches break up the symmetry of this dignified brick facade. The only difference between these mirror-image plans is where the entry is placed. Unit A on the left enters from the side into the family room. The adjacent dining area opens into the kitchen with a snack-bar counter for conversation and casual dining. A pantry and a washer-and-dryer space are conveniently off to the side. A short hallway leads to a half-bath and the master suite, which features a walk-in closet and a private bath. Two bedrooms, a full bath and plenty of closet space make up the second floor. Unit B's entry is at the very front of the building, which slightly increases the square footage of this side.

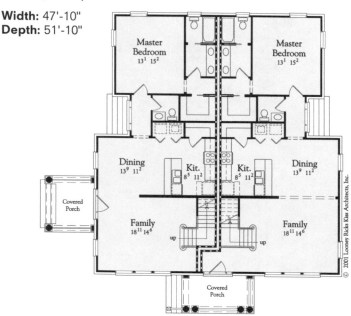

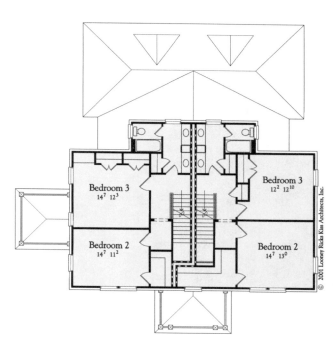

Cressida Place

A hipped roof and a set of distinguished columned porches are the prelude to the elegant layout inside this plan. These twin units delight in open flow between the living and dining areas. Classic multipane windows with shutter accents bring just the right amount of light inside. Tucked away in the back of the plan, the master suite revels in seclusion with its private bath and the biggest walk-in closet in the house. Upstairs, Bedroom 2 is resplendent in windows while Bedroom 3 sits next to the shared full hall bath—featuring a convenient twin-sink vanity.

Plan HPT262003

First Floor: 1,077 sq. ft.
Second Floor: 662 sq. ft.
Total: 1,739 sq. ft. per unit

Width: 47'-10"
Depth: 51'-10"

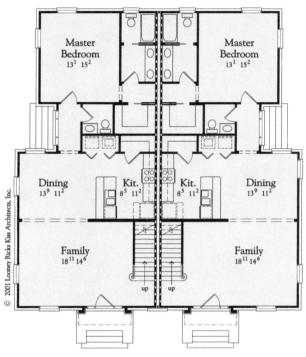

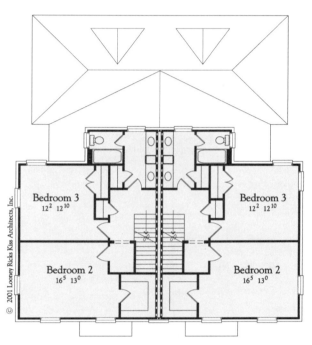

Plan HPT262004

Square Footage: 1,195 per unit

Width: 80'-0"
Depth: 48'-8"

Calle Entrada

The rustic look of shingles combined with country porches give this home's facade a down-home feel. Inside, mirror-image floor plans are perfect for growing families. Step in off the porch into a fine family room. A dining area separates the living space from the C-shaped kitchen in back. The kitchen is equipped with a roomy pantry and opens to a petite porch in back. The sleeping wing lies opposite the living area, consisting of three bedrooms and a convenient laundry room that opens to the two-car garage. The master suite delights with its own private bath, while the two secondary bedrooms share a hall bath. All three bedrooms have ample closet space.

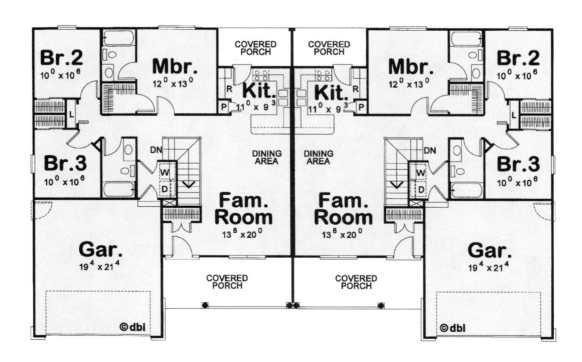

Plan HPT262005

Square Footage: 1,195 per unit

Width: 80'-0"
Depth: 48'-8"

The Snow Maiden

Craftsman appeal takes center stage on this home's facade, with shingles, dormers and pillared porches. Two units inside match one another room-for-room. Open flow between the family room, dining area and kitchen is designed for family convenience. A laundry room opens from the hallway and out to the two-car garage. The spacious master suite has its own private bath and a walk-in closet. Bedrooms 2 and 3 share a hall bath and are met with a handy linen cupboard. A closet in the foyer and a smaller porch out back complete the plan.

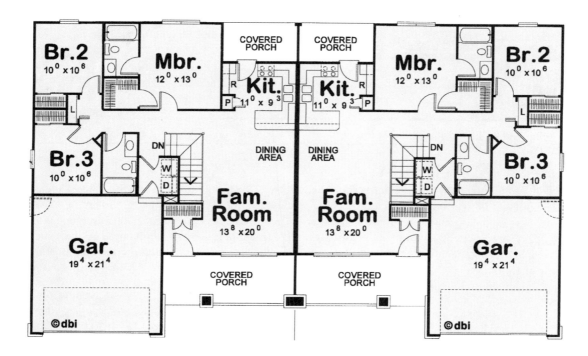

Plan HPT262006

Unit A
Square Footage: 1,335
Unit B
Square Footage: 1,407

Width: 70'-0"
Depth: 62'-3"

Gilded Way

With its shingles and siding and weathervane rooftop accent, this duplex has a bit of a farmhouse feel, but its clean lines make it suitable for any neighborhood. Unit A on the left opens from its entry porch into a sizable living room, complete with a fireplace. Pass through here into the dining area, which is adjacent to the island kitchen and also leads out to a petite covered patio. A hallway leads to a utility room, two closets, a full bath and two bedrooms. Bedroom 2 has its own walk-in closet and features private access to the hall bath. The master suite has a gorgeous skylit bath and an enormous walk-in closet. Unit B on the right opens into a foyer, which leads to the hearth-warmed living room on the right and Bedroom 2 on the left. A full bath is straight ahead. To the left of the living room, the adjacent dining room opens to the galley kitchen. The master suite in this unit has an even larger walk-in closet, and is accented by a tray ceiling. A back patio and a utility room round out this plan.

Wisteria Crossing

It's all in the details for this elegant duplex. Both units are decked out with the best amenities and fine touches throughout. Unit A on the left has three bedrooms—or make one a study. The spacious entry leads to a huge living room, complete with a fireplace and access to a side patio. The living room opens to the dining area, which flows right into the skylit kitchen. A spacious pantry, utility room, and garage access fill out the kitchen. In the back of the plan lie Bedroom 2, equipped with a roomy closet, and the master suite, which is the height of luxury with its vaulted ceiling and stunning private bath. The skylit bath features an enormous walk-in closet, a twin-sink vanity and a compartmented shower and tub. Unit B on the right has virtually all the same features, but in a slightly different layout. The living room is to the back of the plan, while the dining room and Bedroom 2 sit to the left of the entry foyer. The master bath features an angled closet complete with a built-in chest.

Plan HPT262007

Unit A
Square Footage: 1,540
Unit B
Square Footage: 1,619

Width: 70'-0"
Depth: 70'-0"

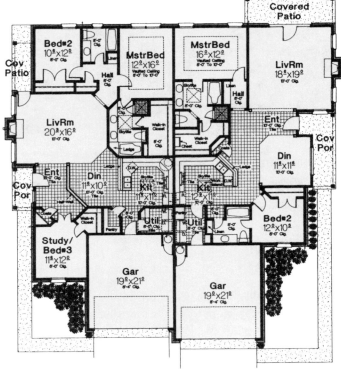

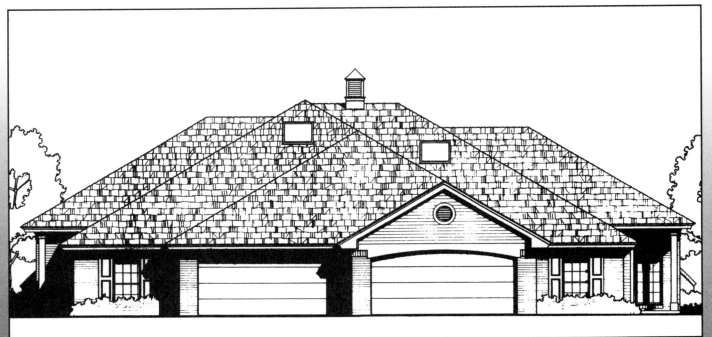

Plan HPT260023

Unit A
Square Footage: 1,825
Unit B
Square Footage: 1,678

Width: 111'-4"
Depth: 50'-0"

Jana Cove

This stylish duplex design offers two slightly altered floor plans for two families. One unit features a covered front porch that welcomes you inside to a foyer, a great room warmed by a fireplace and a dining room. The island kitchen is set between the breakfast room and laundry room, connecting to the two-car garage. Three family bedrooms are placed on the opposite side of the great room, including a master suite with a private bath and walk-in closet. The second unit features an almost mirror-image layout with a central great room also warmed by a fireplace. Family bedrooms are located to one side, while casual living areas are located on the opposite side. This plan is also completed by a two-car garage.

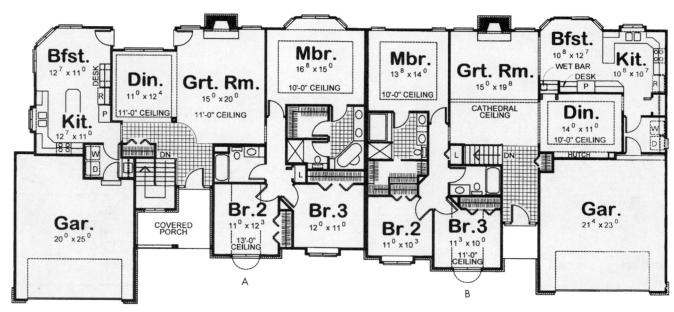

Lienne Pointe

This duplex home, dazzled in traditional and European accents, features two family units boasting stunning amenities. The two units vary slightly in layout. One unit begins with a foyer opening to a dining and great room. A two-sided fireplace warms this great room and a hearth room. Nearby, a kitchen opens to the breakfast room. The master suite is privately secluded, while two additional bedrooms on the opposite side of this layout share a hall bath. The second unit enters directly into the great room with a fireplace from the foyer. The master bedroom and two secondary bedrooms are clustered together on one side, while the island kitchen, breakfast nook and dining area are grouped together on the opposite side. Both units are finished by a two-car family garage.

Plan HPT260024

Unit A
Square Footage: 1,802
Unit B
Square Footage: 1,768

Width: 109'-4"
Depth: 59'-4"

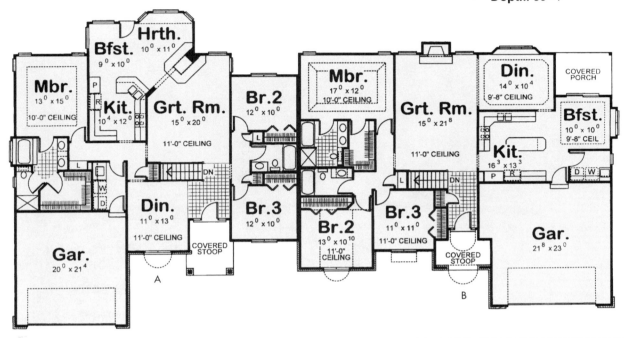

B

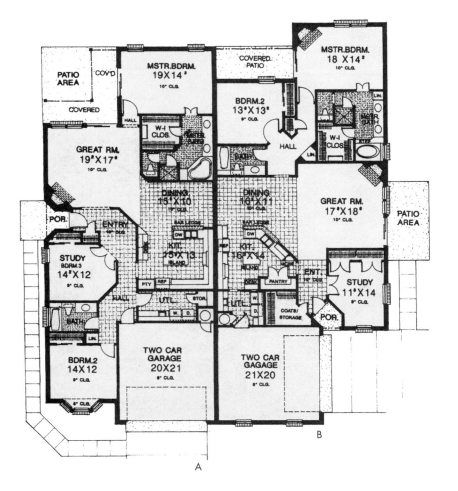

A

Plan HPT260025

Unit A
Square Footage: 2,009
Unit B
Square Footage: 1,997

Width: 68'-10"
Depth: 84'-10"

Belmont Square

This attractive duplex duo provides two separate floor plans which differ slightly. Each unit offers a great room that is warmed by a corner fireplace and accesses an outdoor patio area. Each island kitchen connects to a tiled dining area. Each master bedroom provides a walk-in closet and a private bath. One master bedroom offers a romantic corner fireplace just for two. The additional family bedroom will share the full hall bath with the study, which may be converted into a third family bedroom as space is needed. Both units are completed by a two-car garage.

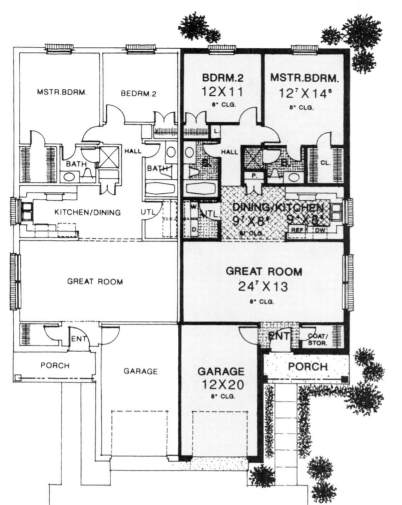

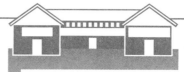

Plan HPT262008

Square Footage: 1,084 per unit

Width: 50'-0"
Depth: 62'-10"

Peony Cottage

This unique plan looks like it might be a single-family home from the outside, but it actually houses two efficient twin units. Enter from the petite front porch to the foyer with its roomy coat closet. Straight ahead is the huge great room, which leads right into the kitchen/dining area. Washer-and-dryer space and a pantry add to the convenience of this space. A short hallway leads to a full bath and two bedrooms. The master suite features a private bath and a spacious walk-in closet. Bedroom 2 is outfitted with its own closet space.

Plan HPT260027

Unit A
Square Footage: 1,255
Unit B
Square Footage: 1,179

Width: 59'-8"
Depth: 74'-0"

West Sunset Ridge

This duplex design provides two stylish options. Unit A enters from the front into the great room, while Unit B enters through the foyer from the side. Both units provide great rooms with fireplaces, kitchens and dining areas, laundry rooms and single-car garages. Each unit offers a master suite with a private bath and walk-in closet and an additional bedroom located near a hall bath. Unit A offers a private patio outside the master suite, while Unit B offers a covered patio accessed from the master bedroom and dining area.

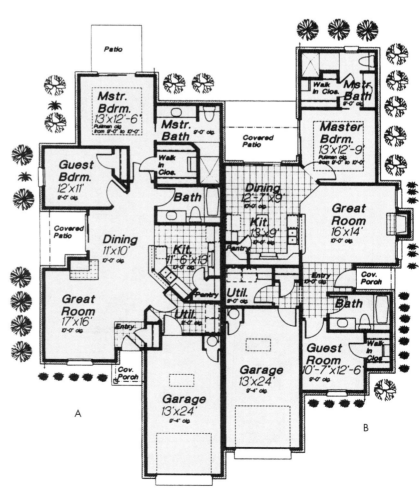

Burleigh Court

This quaint and traditional one-story design features two units with slightly altered floor plans. A library is found to the immediate left of the entry of Unit A. Straight ahead, the formal living room is warmed by a fireplace and opens to the dining room. The kitchen features a nook, while the laundry room connects into the two-car garage. The master bedroom provides a private bath, and Bedroom 2 uses a hall bath nearby. Unit B offers formal living areas, a kitchen with a nook, and two family bedrooms, along with a two-car garage. Both units feature rear screened porches—perfect for outdoor meals in the summertime.

Plan HPT260028

Unit A
Square Footage: 2,006
Unit B
Square Footage: 1,661

Width: 93'-4"
Depth: 67'-0"

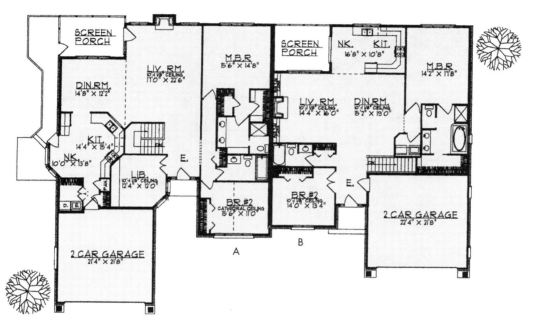

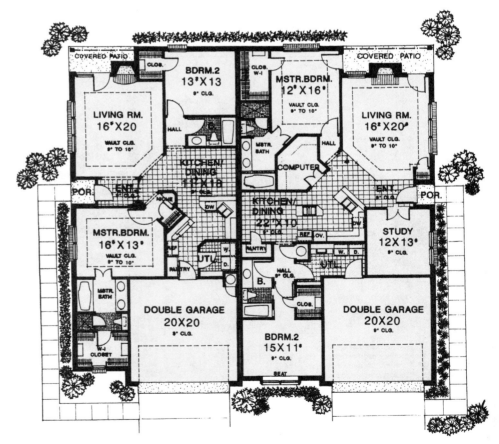

Plan HPT262009

Unit A
Square Footage: 1,435
Unit B
Square Footage: 1,746

Width: 65'-0"
Depth: 64'-10"

Camino Cartamo

This duplex plan has a traditional facade, with heightened rooflines to add a sense of drama. In both units, the kitchen/dining area is the hub of the plan, with the hearth-warmed living room off to the side and opening to a back covered patio. Unit A on the left puts the master suite up front, with its spacious private bath nestled against the garage. Bedroom 2 is in back, right next to a full hall bath. Unit B on the left also has two bedrooms, but keeps the master suite in back while Bedroom 2 takes its place beside the garage. An added bonus on this side is the study, which opens to the left of the foyer. The island kitchen opens into a handy computer space. Both units have two-car garages.

Plan HPT260030

Unit A
Square Footage: 1,775
Unit B
Square Footage: 1,770

Width: 68'-10"
Depth: 75'-3"

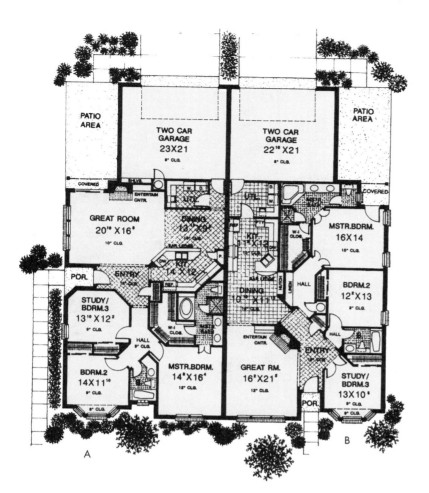

Fitzgerald Place

This stylish duplex offers a traditional silhouette with elegant French touches. Two layouts with slightly different floor plans are provided for two small families. Enter one unit from the front and the second unit from the side—lending a little more privacy to each family. Each unit offers a great room with a fireplace, a kitchen and dining area, a laundry room and three family bedrooms. Each master bedroom features a private bath and a walk-in closet, while the additional two bedrooms share a hall bath. The third bedroom in each option can convert to a study. A two-car garage and outdoor patio complete each unit.

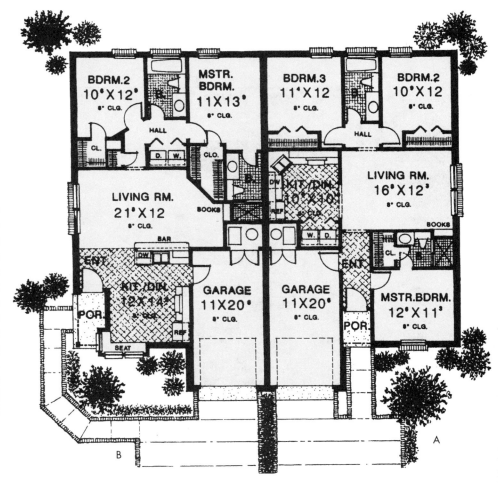

Plan HPT260031

Unit A
Square Footage: 1,040
Unit B
Square Footage: 1,023

Width: 55'-10"
Depth: 50'-10"

Kauffman Circle

This duplex family design offers two cozy layouts for a new or growing family. Unit A provides a three-bedroom option with the master bedroom enjoying a private bath and walk-in closet. Unit B provides a two-bedroom option—both bedrooms offer a walk-in closet and the master suite has a private bath. Each unit enjoys a living room, a kitchen with an eating area, a hall bath and laundry room. Both plans feature a single-car garage, which is conveniently placed near the kitchen for easy loading and unloading.

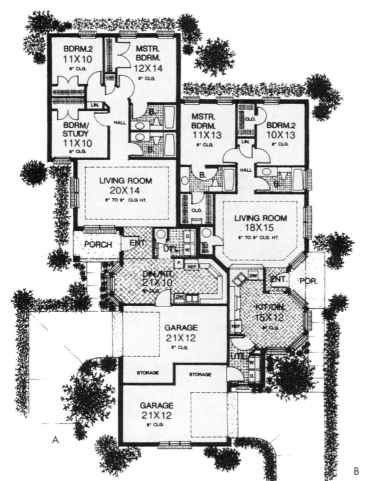

Plan HPT260032

Unit A
Square Footage: 1,229
Unit B
Square Footage: 1,107

Width: 50'-10"
Depth: 83'-2"

Kennedy Cottage

This traditional multi-family home offers two units with slightly different floor plans. Each unit may be entered through the single-car garage or the entry flanked by the kitchen and formal living room. Unit A features a master bedroom with a private bath and two additional bedrooms that share a full hall bath. Unit B is designed for a new family—offering a master bedroom with a walk-in closet and one additional bedroom nearby that also provides a walk-in closet. The master arrangement enjoys a private bath, while Bedroom 2 may use the hall bath located nearby. Each unit is completed by a convenient laundry room and both single-car garages offer additional storage space.

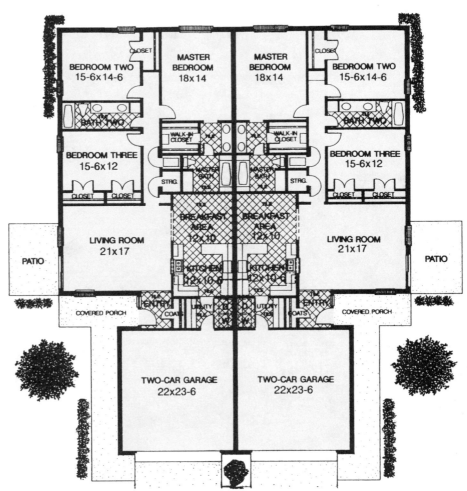

Plan HPT260033

Square Footage:
1,858 per unit

Width: 66'-10"
Depth: 82'-7"

Tazwell Bend

This traditional duplex design features mirror-image units that are perfect for a small or growing family. Enter from the front covered porch into the spacious living room. The kitchen opens to an eating area and connects on the other side through the utility room to the two-car garage. A grilling porch outside of the living room is perfect for summertime barbecues. The master bedroom features a walk-in closet and a private bath. Two additional family bedrooms share a full hall bath located between them.

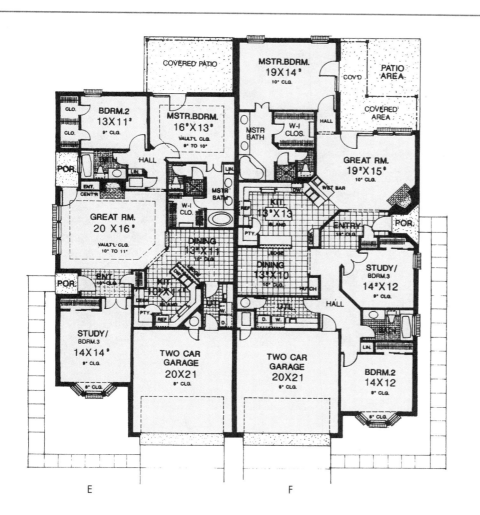

Plan HPT260034

Unit E
Square Footage: 1,967
Unit F
Square Footage: 1,755

Width: 68'-10"
Depth: 79'-10"

Drew's Pointe

Traditional style outlines this favorite duplex design—perfect for growing families. Each unit may be entered from the side or from the two-car garage—placed just outside the laundry room. Although the plans differ slightly in layout, each provides an island kitchen/dining area and a great room warmed by a fireplace. The master bedroom of each plan features a private bath and walk-in closet. The master suite of Unit E enjoys a private covered patio, while the patio of Unit F is accessed from both the master suite and the great room. The two additional bedrooms of each unit share a hall bath—the third bedroom converts to an optional study.

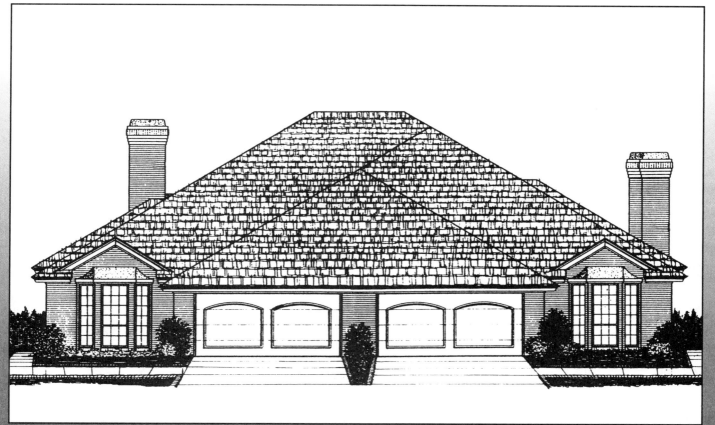

Plan HPT260035

Unit A
Square Footage: 1,781
Unit B
Square Footage: 2,215

Width: 102'-0"
Depth: 77'-0"

Elizabeth Drive

This traditional duplex plan with European accents offers two slightly different floor plans. Unit A enters into the spacious great room, which is warmed by a corner fireplace. The island kitchen features a nook and is well placed between the laundry room that connects to the two-car garage, and the dining room that accesses the rear screened porch. The master suite enjoys a walk-in closet and a private bath. Bedroom 2 uses a hall bath nearby. Unit B offers a couple extra additions to the floor plan, including a wood deck just off the rear screened porch and a study just off the entry. The study can be converted to a third bedroom as space is needed.

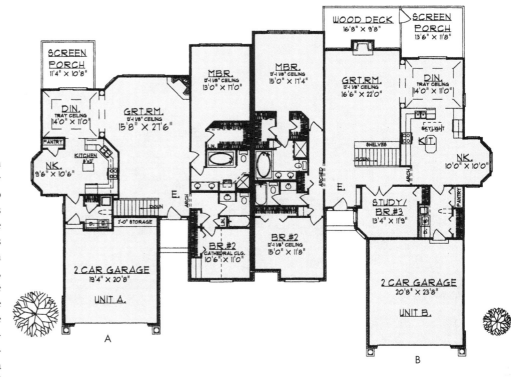

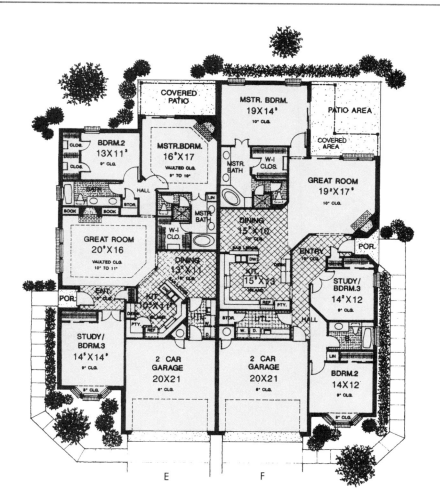

E   F

Plan HPT260036

Unit E
Square Footage: 1,847
Unit F
Square Footage: 1,997

Width: 68'-10"
Depth: 79'-10"

Vineyard's Grove

This stunning duplex home offers a traditional floor plan dazzled in transitional accents. The two units vary slightly—enter either from the two-car garage or a side entrance. Each unit provides a kitchen/dining area, a great room warmed by a fireplace, a laundry room and a hall bath. Each unit provides a sumptuous master bedroom with a private bath and large walk-in closet. Two additional bedrooms are also included—the third bedroom converts to a study. One duplex option allows for a private fireplace in the master suite, while the other option provides for a more spacious outdoor patio.

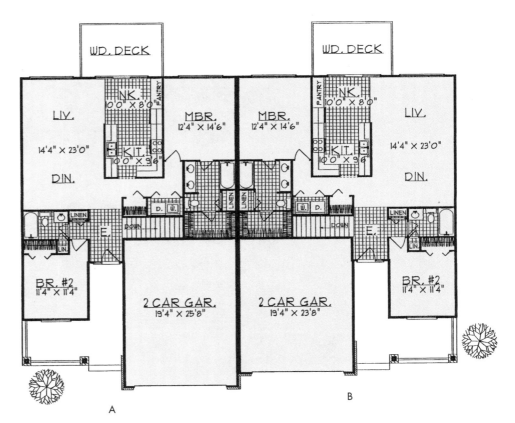

Plan HPT260037

Square Footage:
1,300 per unit

Width: 76'-0"
Depth: 55'-0"

Brandy Falls Avenue

This attractive duplex is perfectly designed for the family just starting out, or the empty-nesters who need less room now that the kids are grown and gone. The units mirror one another and have many amenities to offer. A spacious living area encompasses both the living room as well as a dining area, and is conveniently located near to the efficient kitchen. A wooden deck just outside the breakfast nook provides a place for dining alfresco. The master bedroom is complete with a dual lavatory and a walk-in closet. The front bedroom—or make it a cozy study—enjoys a full bath and two linen closets available nearby.

Cortesi Circle

Two gables adorn the front of this fine duplex, while inside, matching units offer a place to call home. The foyer opens directly into the living area where there is space for both a living room and a dining area. The open kitchen offers a cheerful pass-through to the dining area. Here, sliding glass doors access the side yard, letting natural light flood the area. Two bedrooms share a full hall bath which features both a shower as well as a tub. The one-car garage offers some storage for yard equipment. This home is designed with a basement foundation.

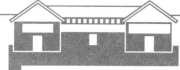

Plan HPT260038

Square Footage: 834 per unit

Width: 48'-0"
Depth: 44'-0"

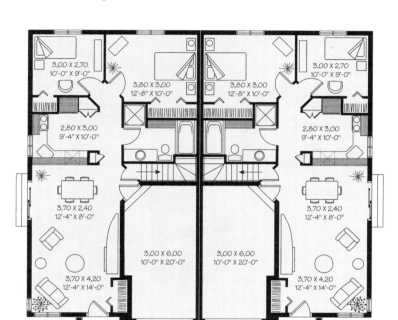

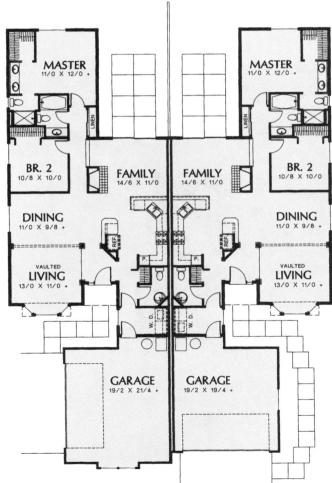

Plan HPT260039

Square Footage:
1,367 per unit

Width: 60'-0"
Depth: 83'-0"

Ashleigh Meadows

With the two-car garages facing different directions, this duplex might easily pass for a single family unit at first glance. Inside, however, the layouts are identical, with many amenities. The master suite is large and comfortable, offering a walk-in closet and a private bath. There is a formal area for entertaining, with the living room featuring a vaulted ceiling and a bay window. A family room is available in which to relax—complete with a fireplace. The large kitchen is easily accessible to both the dining room and the family room, providing ease of service.

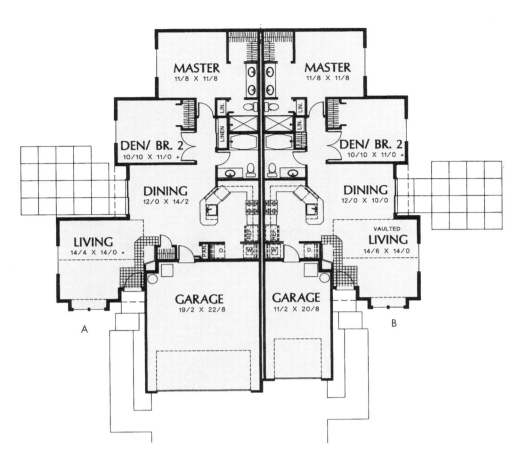

Plan HPT260040

Unit A
Square Footage: 1,115
Unit B
Square Footage: 1,052

Width: 62'-0"
Depth: 64'-0"

Brandon's Way

The only big difference between these two attractive units is the garage. Unit A offers a two-car garage to complement its interior, while Unit B provides a one-car garage. Both units feature a spacious living room with a fireplace and a box-bay window. The angled kitchen offers a peninsula with a sink and provides easy service to the dining room. Here, a patio awaits to accommodate dining alfresco. The master suite is complete with a walk-in closet and a private bath. The den—or make it a second bedroom—enjoys access to a large linen closet as well as a full hall bath.

Plan HPT262010

Square Footage: 422 per unit

Width: 48'-0"
Depth: 47'-0"

Petunia Garden

At first glance, this duplex might look like just a deluxe garage—but it actually holds two compact apartments! Great for in-laws, grown-up kids or bringing in some extra income, these one-bedroom beauties sit behind a spacious garage. Though they are small, these units are outfitted with some luxury amenities, such as a bay-windowed kitchen and a hearth-warmed living room. But the best bonus of all might be the spacious rear deck, which is accessed through sliding glass doors in the living room. A shower bath and a roomy coat closet in the foyer complete the plan.

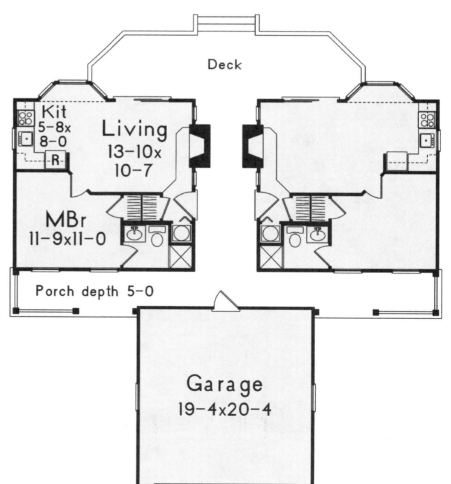

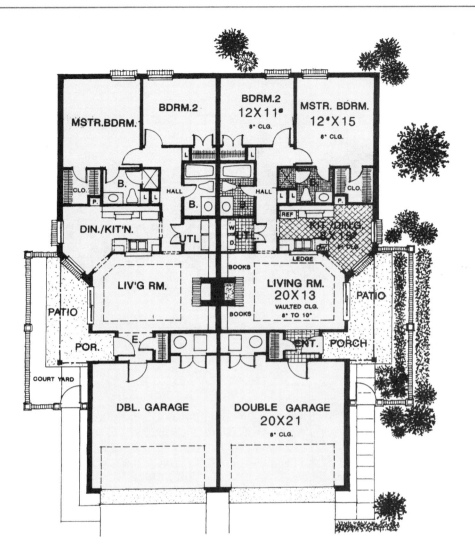

Plan HPT262011

Square Footage: 1,057 per unit

Width: 50'-0"
Depth: 68'-10"

The Wellspring

A set of two-car garages hides the two family-size homes in this classy duplex. Each unit begins with a sweet patio-and-porch combination, opening into an entry foyer that can also be accessed from the garage. From here, enter the living room, made luxurious by a tray ceiling and cozy fireplace. The kitchen/dining area looks over to the living room from a pass-through above the sink. A hallway from the kitchen leads to the utility room, a full bath and two bedrooms. The master suite features a walk-in closet and a private bath. Bedroom 2 has its own spacious closet. The double-garage "decoy" also provides added privacy and security.

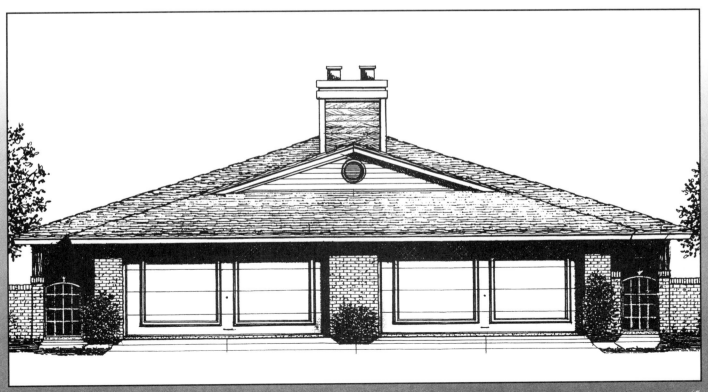

Plan HPT260043

Square Footage: 828 per unit

Width: 72'-0"
Depth: 38'-0"

Sterling Hollow

Easy one-story livability is the attraction of this lovely duplex design. Mirror-image floor plans reside back to back. Petite covered porches open into the living room of each unit. The living room, which views the front property, also accesses the rear patio—great for grilling or refreshing outdoor entertainment. The compact yet efficient kitchen opens to the dining area, overlooking the front porch. The two family bedrooms share a full hall bath—perfect for empty-nesters or young families. Please specify crawlspace or slab foundation when ordering.

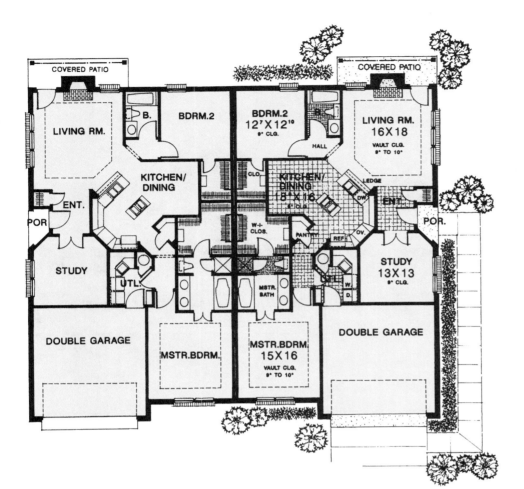

Plan HPT262012

Square Footage: 1,635 per unit

Width: 70'-0"
Depth: 61'-10"

Harvest Moon

Tudor accents gussy up the facade of this charming duplex. Each of the twin plans has its own two-car garage and covered back patio. You can enter the home through either the garage or the side-porch entry, which opens into a foyer with a handy coat closet. The foyer in turn opens to the huge living room, accented with a vaulted ceiling and a fireplace, as well as access to the back patio. The living room flows into the kitchen/dining area, which features a pantry and the utility room, and leads back into a short hallway to the master suite. The master bath has a separate tub and shower and a gigantic walk-in closet fit for royalty. Bedroom 2 in the back of the plan also has its own walk-in closet and utilizes the full hall bath.

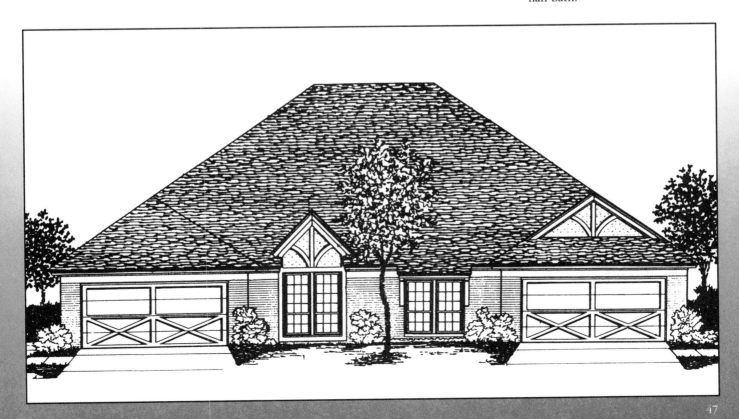

Plan HPT260045

Square Footage: 850 per unit

Width: 68'-0"
Depth: 37'-0"

St. Jeanine Avenue

This attractive duplex home is enhanced by stylish symmetry and mirror image floor plans. Country dormers and porches welcome you inside to a vaulted living area. The vaulted space continues into the combined kitchen and dining area. The U-shape of the kitchen allows for compact efficiency. Bedroom 1 provides impressive closet space, while Bedroom 2 is perfect for a nursery or home office—great for young couples just starting out or empty-nesters. The two bedrooms share a full hall bath. Each unit offers a single-car garage.

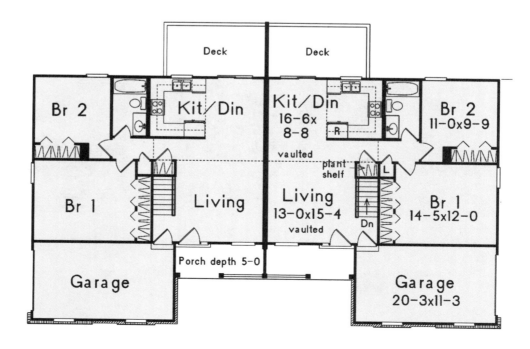

Stonewood Cottage

This peaceful suburban duplex features a traditional rustic look, which blends easily into any countryside setting. The units mirror each other starting with quaint front covered porches, single-car garages and a family-efficient floor plan. Each plan features a petite kitchen area connecting to a dining room, overlooking a patio—perfect for outdoor grilling. The vaulted great room is warmed by a fireplace and has a spacious feel. A staircase in the foyer leads to an optional basement plan. Bedrooms 2 and 3 share a full hall bath, while the master suite enjoys a walk-in closet and a private bath.

Plan HPT260046

Square Footage:
1,159 per unit

Width: 80'-0"
Depth: 42'-8"

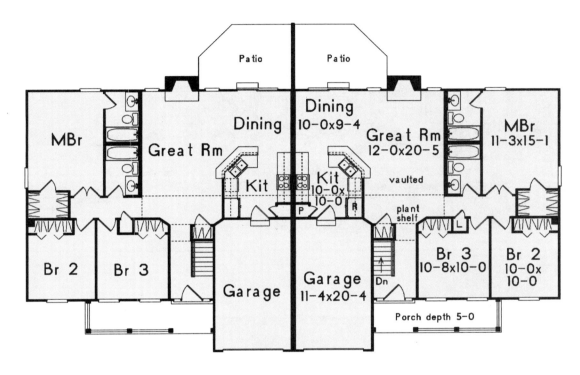

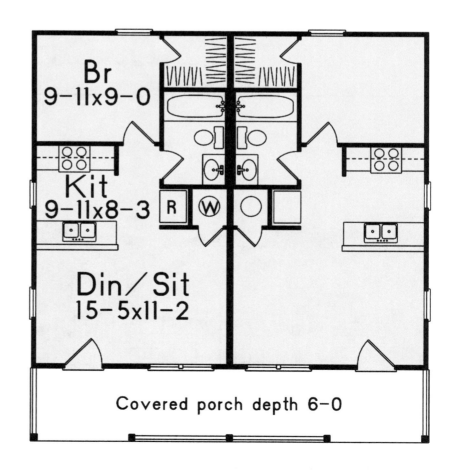

Plan HPT262013

Square Footage: 448 per unit

Width: 32'-0"
Depth: 34'-0"

Rockville Road

This sweet little cabin makes the perfect vacation spot for outdoor enthusiasts! A carefree layout has all the necessities—full kitchen, roomy living room, a bedroom with plenty of closet space and a full bath. Windows all around let you take in nature's wonder. The front porch is ideal for outdoor dining and stargazing on cool evenings. Share this duplex with your favorite friends or make it a treasured family retreat.

Br
9-11x9-0

Kit
9-11x8-3

R W

Din/Sit
15-5x11-2

Covered porch depth 6-0

Butterfly Ridge

This country ranch duplex takes vacation living to the next level. Two bedrooms, both with roomy closets, give everyone privacy while the living and dining areas are set up for socializing. The spacious front porch brings the outdoors in, while the door to the rear property is ideal for slipping out for impromptu walks. Space for a washer-and-dryer set means you won't be "roughing it" too hard! A full hall bath and linen storage finish off these mirror-image plans.

Plan HPT262014

Square Footage: 768 per unit

Width: 32'-0"
Depth: 24'-0"

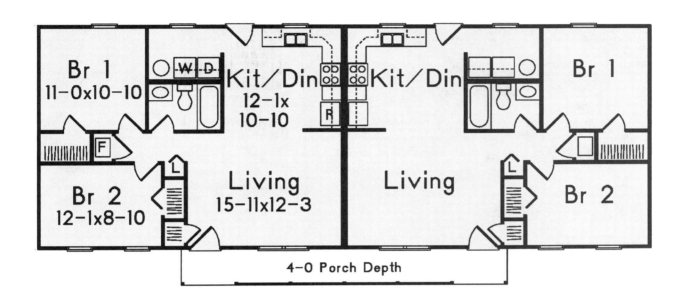

Plan HPT260049

Unit A
Square Footage: 1,259
Finished Basement: 870
Unit B
Square Footage: 1,540
Finished Basement: 683

Width: 85'-8"
Depth: 59'-8"

Kristin Falls

This duplex design offers two levels of
livability for the growing family. The
main level of each unit features two
family bedrooms, two baths, a
kitchen, a dining area and the great
room warmed by a fireplace. Laundry
closets in each home are large enough
for a washer and dryer. The main level
of each unit is completed by a wood
deck—perfect for outdoor grilling in
the summertime—and a two-car
garage. The lower level features a
third bedroom, a recreation room,
storage space and unexcavated space.

Sarah Francis Lane

This one-story duplex home features slightly different floor plans. Unit A provides a charming front covered porch, which enters inside to the kitchen/nook area immediately on the left. A two-car garage is located to the right. The great room accesses a rear deck and is open to the dining area. The master bedroom offers a private bath and walk-in closet. A hall bath is located just across the hall from Bedroom 2. The entryway of Unit B is flanked by Bedroom 2 and a hall bath on one side and the two-car garage on the left. Again, the great room and dining area are open to each other. The kitchen opens to a nook overlooking the rear deck.

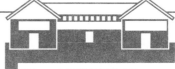

Plan HPT260050

Unit A
Square Footage: 1,247
Unit B
Square Footage: 1,253

Width: 79'-4"
Depth: 50'-0"

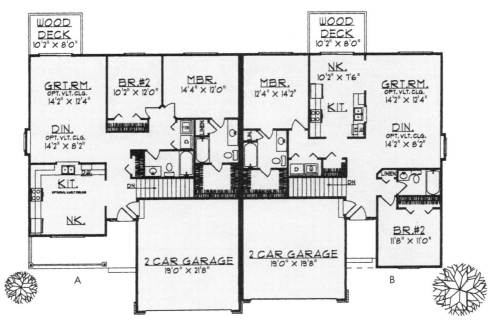

Plan HPT260051

Unit A
Square Footage: 1,212
Unit B
Square Footage: 1,233

Width: 80'-0"
Depth: 47'-8"

Monet Falls

Everything people want in a single-family starter home is featured in this duplex home that's perfect for singles or small families. The large great room features a fireplace, transoms and built-in shelves. The modern kitchen provides a separate breakfast area and snack counter. The master suite is pampering with a walk-in closet and private bath. The second bedroom is placed near a hall bath and linen closet. Extras include a two-car garage accessed through the laundry room and tons of closet space—especially in the master suite!

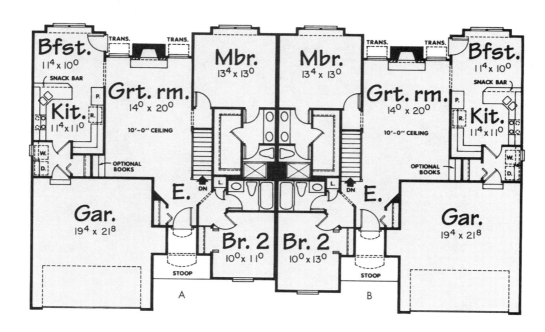

Lindsey Lane

This duplex home provides two separate units with mirror-image floor plans. Exterior materials create an optional brick or siding facade, while abundant windows fill the interior with light. Each one-story unit enters the apartment through a petite front covered porch into the living room. This room accesses the rear patio, which is perfect for outdoor dining and stargazing. The efficient kitchen is open to the dining area. Two family bedrooms share a full hall bath. Please specify crawlspace or slab foundation when ordering.

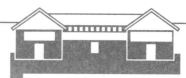

Plan HPT260052

Square Footage: 828 per unit

Width: 72'-0"
Depth: 38'-0"

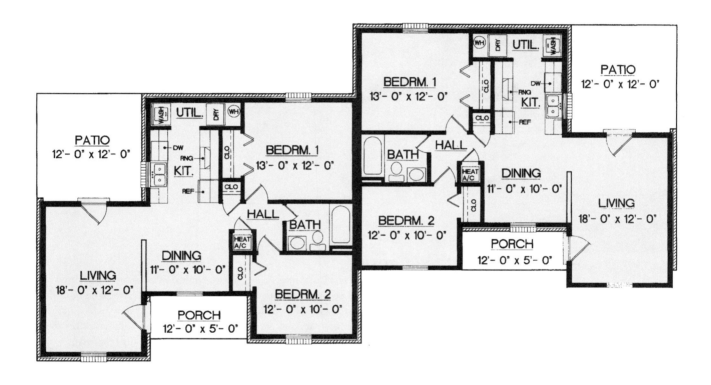

PATIO
12'- 0" x 12'- 0"

UTIL.

KIT.

BEDRM. 1
13'- 0" x 12'- 0"

HALL

BATH

DINING
11'- 0" x 10'- 0"

LIVING
18'- 0" x 12'- 0"

PORCH
12'- 0" x 5'- 0"

BEDRM. 2
12'- 0" x 10'- 0"

BEDRM. 1
13'- 0" x 12'- 0"

UTIL.

KIT.

PATIO
12'- 0" x 12'- 0"

BATH

HALL

BEDRM. 2
12'- 0" x 10'- 0"

DINING
11'- 0" x 10'- 0"

LIVING
18'- 0" x 12'- 0"

PORCH
12'- 0" x 5'- 0"

Plan HPT260053

Square Footage: 852 per unit

Width: 76'-0"
Depth: 37'-0"

Bluefield Grove

This country cottage home is a charming and efficient duplex design, economical for any young family. Planter boxes and two covered front porches add a touch of quaint country decor to the exterior. The living room connects to the kitchen, which includes a pantry and a sunny bay window. Access to the single-car garage and the rear patio are conveniently placed nearby. The master bedroom, which features a walk-in closet, and Bedroom 2 share a full hall bath and a hall linen closet.

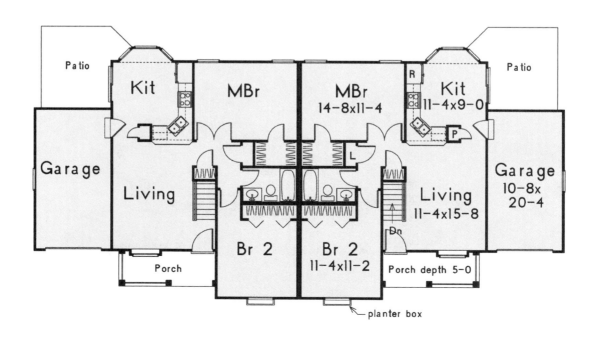

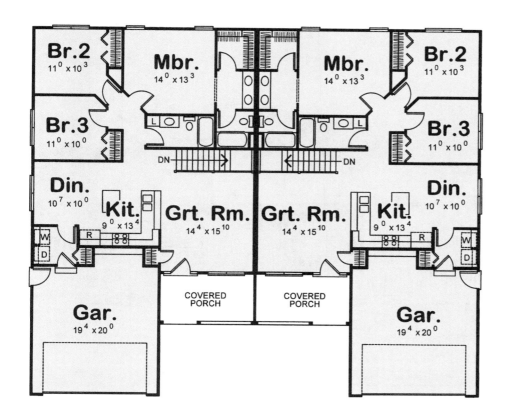

Plan HPT260054

Square Footage:
1,311 per unit

Width: 69'-4"
Depth: 58'-4"

Hillary Hollow

Mirror-image floor plans comfortably accommodate two families in this traditional duplex plan. Covered front porches welcome you inside to a great room. The island kitchen opens to a dining area, which connects through the laundry room to the two-car garage. The master bedroom suite features a spacious walk-in closet and a private double-bowl vanity bath. Bedrooms 2 and 3 share a full hall bath. Bedroom 3 is perfect for a home office for the family entrepreneur who wants to work at home.

Plan HPT260055

Square Footage: 676 per unit

Width: 52'-0"
Depth: 32'-0"

Mt. Kimberly Road

This enchanting rustic design is a perfect duplex for empty-nesters or seasonal vacationers. The exterior and interior layout are ideal for a countryside, lakeside or serene mountain setting—perfect for couples or young families looking for a quiet escape. The long front covered porch welcomes you inside to a combined living and dining area. A storage pantry serves the compact kitchen nearby. The living room shares a two-sided fireplace with the bedroom—a romantic touch for honeymooners. A full hall bathroom is located behind the kitchen.

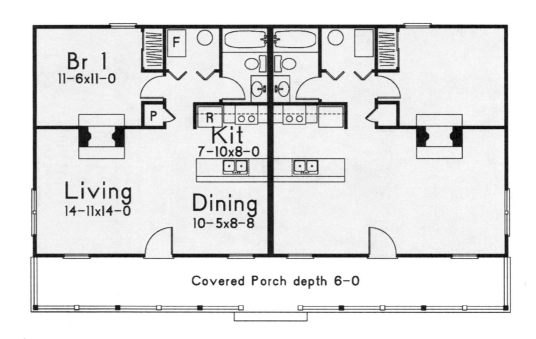

Br 1
11-6x11-0

Kit
7-10x8-0

Living
14-11x14-0

Dining
10-5x8-8

Covered Porch depth 6-0

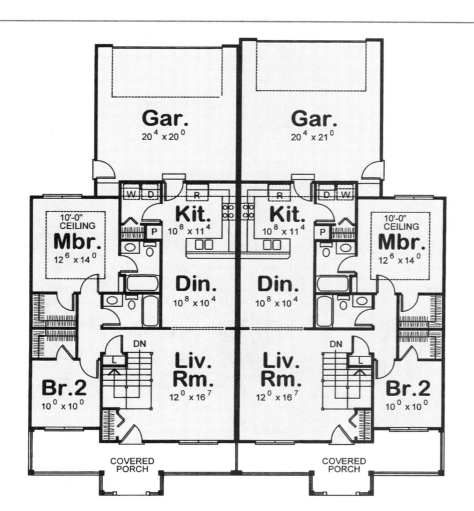

Plan HPT260056

Square Footage:
1,142 per unit

Width: 60'-8"
Depth: 60'-8"

Glenndevon

This one-story duplex plan features efficient mirror-image designs. A long covered front porch welcomes you inside to each unit. The spacious living room is perfect for casual or formal occasions. The kitchen connects to both the dining area and laundry room and directly accesses the rear two-car garage for convenience. Each unit features two family bedrooms, which will comfortably accommodate a young family. The master bedroom offers a walk-in closet and a private bath, while the second bedroom also provides a walk-in closet—a full hall bath is located nearby.

Plan HPT260057

Square Footage:
1,415 per unit

Width: 96'-0"
Depth: 50'-4"

West Lowell Ranch

This traditional duplex design is enhanced by ranch-style features, perfectly suited to most suburban or countryside neighborhoods. From a small front porch, enter inside to a spacious great room straight ahead, warmed by a country fireplace. The nearby kitchen with a pantry overlooks the dining area. A door close by accesses the rear covered porch—ideal for enjoying the sun or outdoor grilling. The master bedroom provides a walk-in closet, a master bath and private access to the rear porch. The secondary bedroom with a walk-in closet is convertible to a den or study for empty-nesters. A full hall bath is located nearby.

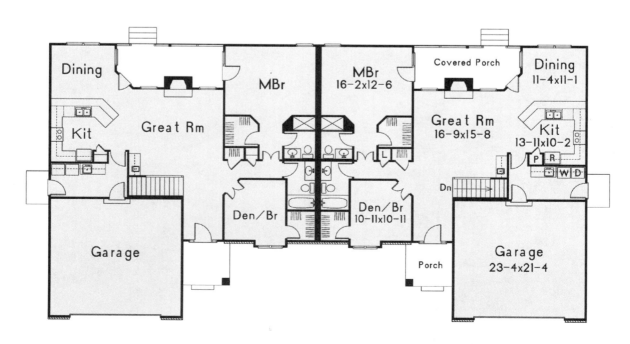

Plan HPT260058

Unit A
Square Footage: 1,492
Unit B
Square Footage: 1,497

Width: 71'-0"
Depth: 61'-0"

Sweet Bea Heights

This delightful duplex plan offers comfortable family living and efficiency. Enter each unit through a petite covered porch that welcomes you into a foyer hall. The corner fireplace warms a vaulted living and dining room. The kitchen provides access to a washroom. The master suite—which is secluded for privacy—offers extensive closet space and a private bath, while two additional family bedrooms on the opposite side of the plan share a full hall bath. Unit A provides a two-car garage, while unit B offers a single-car garage.

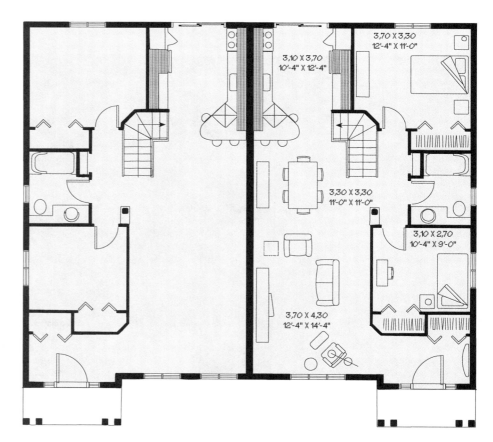

Plan HPT260059

Square Footage:
1,893 per unit

Width: 48'-0"
Depth: 40'-0"

3,70 X 3,30
12'-4" X 11'-0"

3,10 X 3,70
10'-4" X 12'-4"

3,30 X 3,30
11'-0" X 11'-0"

3,10 X 2,70
10'-4" X 9'-0"

3,70 X 4,30
12'-4" X 14'-4"

Campbell Creek Drive

Elegant living can be found in this duplex home. Enhanced with columns and a lovely pediment just above the entryway, this design offers slight differences in facade and window treatments. One side enjoys a circle-top window and an open gable, while the other is understated with a gable roofline. Inside, the floor plans are identical. The open living area provides space for a dining area and entertaining space. The kitchen features a breakfast bar and plenty of counter space. Two bedrooms and a full bath complete this efficient design. This home is designed with a basement foundation.

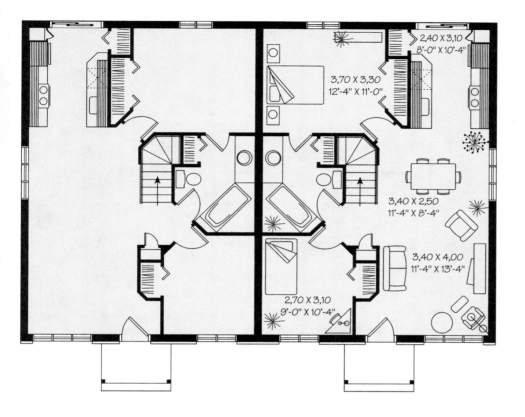

2,40 X 3,10
8'-0" X 10'-4"

3,70 X 3,30
12'-4" X 11'-0"

3,40 X 2,50
11'-4" X 8'-4"

3,40 X 4,00
11'-4" X 13'-4"

2,70 X 3,10
9'-0" X 10'-4"

Plan HPT260060

Square Footage: 816 per unit

Width: 48'-0"
Depth: 34'-0"

Teralyn Drive

This attractive duplex home offers comfortable livability with a convenient one-story elevation. The floor plan is perfect for couples just starting out. A small covered porch welcomes you inside to a casual or formal living room. Here, the room is open to a dining area located close to the kitchen. A storage pantry in the kitchen allows for additional space. The larger family bedroom directly accesses the full bath, while the second bedroom uses the hall entrance to the bath. The second bedroom is also the perfect size for a home office or nursery. This home is designed with a basement foundation.

Plan HPT260061

Square Footage: 996 per unit

Width: 60'-0"
Depth: 55'-0"

Sukaina Circle

Perfectly suited to warmer climates, this beautiful stucco duplex features stunning European and Mediterranean accents. Enter one of the units through the front porch or the single-car garage. The kitchen provides a walk-in pantry, space for a washer and dryer, and a combined dining/great room with a vaulted ceiling warmed by a fireplace. Access the rear patio for outdoor grilling. The master suite features a linen closet, private bath and walk-in closet. The second family bedroom is located near the full hall bath. Designed for the young or growing family, this charming duplex home is both economical and stylish for any neighborhood setting.

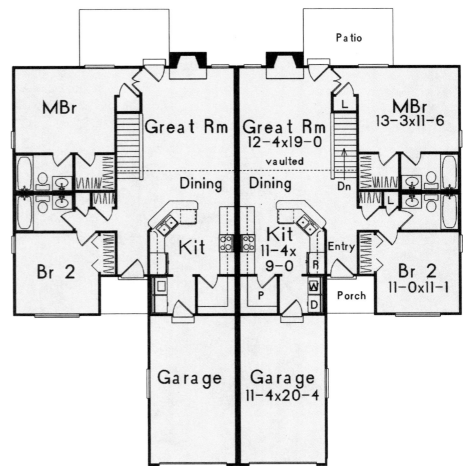

Holland Court

Exquisite French style and other elegant European details add to the appeal of this unique duplex home. French shutters and a stucco facade add to the exterior decor, while mirror-image floor plans flank an exquisite fountain courtyard and central porch. Each apartment is entered from a central foyer. The living room is warmed by a fireplace and accesses a rear porch through a set of double doors. The kitchen connects to both the rear porch and the dining area. The master bedroom offers front-yard views, a walk-in closet and a private full bath. A secondary bedroom is placed near a full hall bath. Please specify crawlspace or slab foundation when ordering.

Plan HPT260062

Square Footage:
1,083 per unit

Width: 70'-0"
Depth: 44'-0"

Plan HPT260063

Unit A
Square Footage: 1,503
Unit B
Square Footage: 637

Width: 59'-8"
Depth: 44'-4"

Blueberry Lane

This unique duplex design offers an attractive yet unusual feature. Double doors enter inside to a foyer that provides a hall closet. The living room with an optional fireplace opens to the dining area and island kitchen. A hallway leads to three family bedrooms, which all share a pampering hall bath. A door at the end of the hallway or to the right of the front entrance, accesses the attached single-bedroom apartment—perfect for a college student, an elderly relative or the in-laws. This attached unit features a kitchen area with its own dining and living rooms, a hall bath and even its own foyer. This home is designed with a basement foundation.

Plan HPT260064

Unit A
First Floor: 852 sq. ft.
Second Floor: 1,032 sq. ft.
Total: 1,884 sq. ft.
Unit B
Square Footage: 588

Width: 38'-0"
Depth: 38'-0"

Jasmine Boulevard

This unique European design with Mediterranean-inspired accents features a duplex addition for today's extended family. Double doors enter into a foyer accessing two separate living spaces. The combined living and dining area of the main house is illuminated by a bay window and introduces a spectacular staircase to the second floor. Beyond this living area, the island snack bar in the kitchen overlooks a nook, located near a powder/laundry room. The first-floor apartment, with a second access behind the staircase, offers a living/dining area, kitchen, bedroom, private bath and laundry closet—great for elderly relatives or a college student. Three family bedrooms and two baths are located upstairs in the main house. This home is designed with a basement foundation.

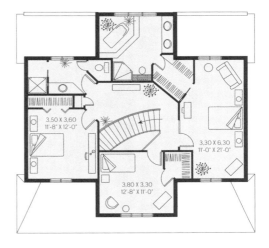

Plan HPT260065

First-Floor Unit: 886 sq. ft.
Second-Floor Unit:
    1,208 sq. ft.

Width: 36'-0"
Depth: 36'-0"

Summerhaven

While the exterior of this house offers the image of a large Victorian-accented home, the interior provides a duplex layout that's perfect for an extended family. A wraparound covered porch hugs the first-floor layout, while an upstairs balcony-deck wraps around the second apartment. Enter into the foyer, which opens inside to the first unit or leads upstairs to the second unit. An island kitchen, living/dining area and three bedrooms sharing a hall bath are provided in the second-floor apartment—great for a young family. Downstairs, a single-bedroom unit also includes a living room, kitchen and hall bath—perfect for an elderly relative. The second-floor apartment features a brilliant bay window, illuminating the master bedroom, while the first-floor apartment offers a single-car garage. This home is designed with a basement foundation.

Joplin Lane

A charming front portico provides an inviting entry into this impressive and symmetrical duplex design. Victorian accents and a formal brick exterior enclose two floor plans. Each unit offers comfortable family living on two floors. The first floor provides a spacious living room and dining area, overlooked by an island kitchen. In unit A the second floor consists of two bedrooms, a large bath and a laundry area, while in unit B, three bedrooms share a full hall bath. The baths include a soaking tub, a separate shower, toilet and vanity sink. This home is designed with a basement foundation.

Plan HPT260066

First Floor: 600 sq. ft.
Second Floor: 600 sq. ft.
Total: 1,200 sq. ft. per unit

Width: 40'-0"
Depth: 30'-0"

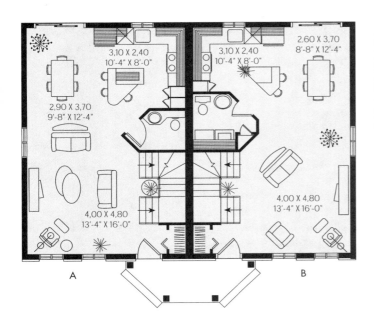

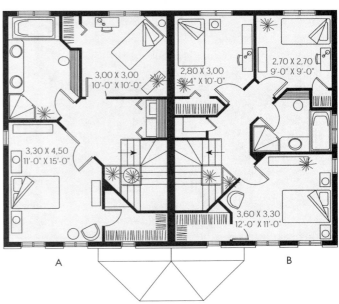

Plan HPT260067

Square Footage: 987 per unit

Width: 32'-4"
Depth: 37'-8"

Cornelia Terrace

This two-story Victorian duplex offers two nearly identical floor plans. The overall design gives the option of a duplex or a triplex. The daylight basement can be used as storage or finished to create a third apartment. All three units are essentially the same, with a living room set in a bay, a dining room, a kitchen opening onto the deck or patio by way of a sliding glass door (except the basement unit), two bedrooms, a full bath and a laundry area. Each apartment enjoys a private entrance. This home is designed with a basement foundation.

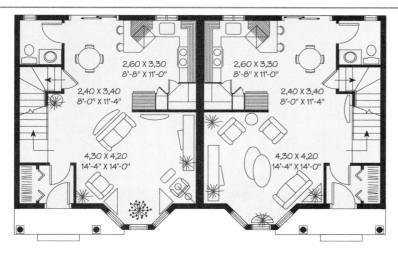

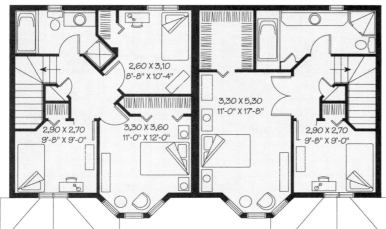

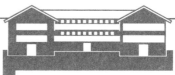

Plan HPT260068

First Floor: 543 sq. ft.
Second Floor: 543 sq. ft.
Total: 1,086 sq. ft. per unit

Width: 44'-0"
Depth: 26'-6"

Bedford Farms

Victorian accents and country style enhance the exterior of this cozy duplex design. Inside, the first-floor layout provides a mirror-image plan of the neighboring apartment. The living room, brightened by a beautiful bay window, is open to the dining area. The U-shaped kitchen provides a handy snack bar. An entry closet and powder room complete the first floor. The second floors of the two units differ slightly. One unit provides a second-floor plan that includes a master bedroom, two additional bedrooms and a hall bath. The other unit plans for a master bedroom with a huge walk-in closet and one additional bedroom—both rooms share a hall bath. This home is designed with a basement foundation.

Plan HPT260069

Unit A
First Floor: 1,097 sq. ft.
Second Floor: 541 sq. ft.
Total: 1,638 sq. ft.
Unit B
First Floor: 1,087 sq. ft.
Second Floor: 616 sq. ft.
Total: 1,703 sq. ft.

Width: 70'-0"
Depth: 41'-0"

Prideaux Park Falls

Gables and dormers grace the exterior of this traditional facade. Slightly different floor plans are provided for each duplex unit. Both units feature two-story living rooms with corner fireplaces. The kitchen opens to a dining area. Each unit includes a utility room, while one of the units has a rear porch. One unit offers a first-floor master suite, while the other provides a first-floor secondary bedroom. Two family bedrooms are offered on the second floor of one unit, while one second-floor bedroom is offered in the other.

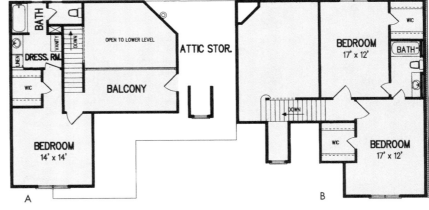

South Groveland

This contemporary duplex design offers two layouts with slight variation. The layout of the first floor offers a mirror-image design of its duplex partner. A side porch enters the unit and leads to the formal living room warmed by a fireplace. The kitchen is open to a dining area overlooking the patio. A secondary bedroom is placed at the front of the plan, with a hall bath nearby. A utility room and single-car garage complete the first floor. The master bedroom with a private bath and walk-in closet dominates the second floor of Unit A. The Unit B option provides a master suite and a third bedroom on the second floor for a slightly larger family.

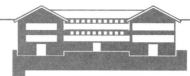

Plan HPT260070

Unit A
First Floor: 1,152 sq. ft.
Second Floor: 428 sq. ft.
Total: 1,580 sq. ft.
Unit B
First Floor: 1,152 sq. ft.
Second Floor: 674 sq. ft.
Total: 1,826 sq. ft.

Width: 70'-10"
Depth: 65'-4"

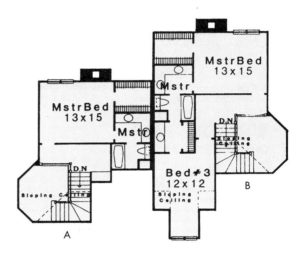

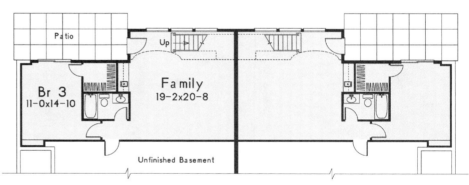

Plan HPT260071

Square Footage:
   1,073 sq. ft. per unit
Finished Basement:
   760 sq. ft. per unit

Width: 81'-0"
Depth: 49'-0"

McClary Cottage

Traditional, serene and totally country, this duplex design is both eye-catching and economically efficient for any family. Dormers, a front covered porch and horizontal siding make a rustic first impression. The front door introduces a combined foyer, which is shared by each unit. Inside, a combined living and dining room is vaulted for a spacious impression. The nearby kitchen features a pantry and overlooks the rear porch. Double doors open into the master bedroom, and all the bedrooms feature walk-in closets. A hall bath and two-car garage with storage complete the main level. Downstairs, the family room shares a hall bath with an additional third bedroom.

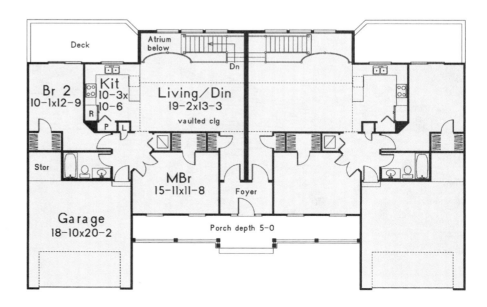

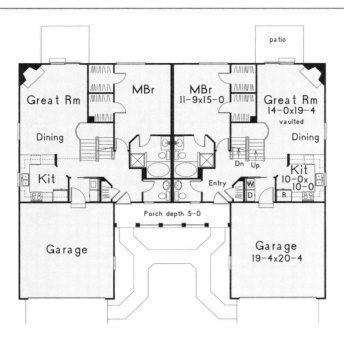

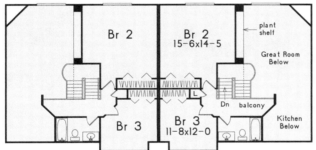

Plan HPT260072

First Floor: 960 sq. ft.
Second Floor: 533 sq. ft.
Total: 1,493 sq. ft. per unit

Width: 64'-0"
Depth: 50'-8"

Chelsea Boulevard

A country front covered porch welcomes you inside to a charming and traditional duplex home. Just inside, a powder room and hall closet flank the foyer. The U-shaped kitchen overlooks the dining area and two-story great room, featuring a fireplace. The first-floor master suite enjoys His and Hers walk-in closets and a private bath. A laundry room connecting to the garage completes the first floor. Upstairs, Bedrooms 2 and 3 share a full hall bath and a balcony hall overlooking the great room and kitchen below.

Plan HPT260073

First-Floor Unit: 1,011 sq. ft.
Second-Floor Unit: 1,018 sq. ft.

Width: 32'-0"
Depth: 32'-0"

Kentucky Grove

This contemporary country design features two units just right for two young families. Each unit provides a spacious family room—great for casual or formal occasions. The living space expands into the dining area—opposite of the kitchen, which features a snack bar counter. Each unit provides two family bedrooms—the master bedroom is located at the rear, while the secondary bedroom offers front-yard views. This room is perfect for a nursery or home office. Both bedrooms share a full hall bath. This home is designed with a basement foundation.

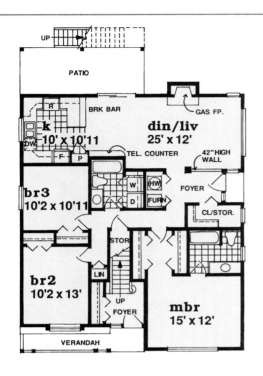

PATIO

UP

R
k
10' x 10'11
DW
F   P
BRK BAR

din/liv
25' x 12'

GAS FP.

TEL. COUNTER

42" HIGH WALL

FOYER

W   HW
D   FURN

CL/STOR.

br3
10'2 x 10'11

STOR

LN

UP FOYER

br2
10'2 x 13'

UP

mbr
15' x 12'

VERANDAH

Plan HPT260074

First-Floor Unit: 1,453 sq. ft.
Second-Floor Unit: 1,438 sq. ft.

Width: 36'-0"
Depth: 43'-0"

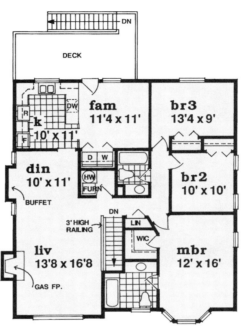

DN

DECK

R
k
10' x 11'
F
DW

fam
11'4 x 11'

br3
13'4 x 9'

D   W

din
10' x 11'

HW
FURN

br2
10' x 10'

BUFFET

3' HIGH RAILING

DN

LIN

WIC

liv
13'8 x 16'8

mbr
12' x 16'

GAS FP.

Magee Square

This economical two-story duplex provides great curb appeal and plenty of space. The first floor features a 1,453 square foot unit with three bedrooms, a U-shaped kitchen and two full baths. The living/dining room is warmed by a gas fireplace and boasts a half-wall overlooking the rear foyer. The second floor offers a self-contained 1,438 square foot unit, also with three bedrooms. Here, a living room with a gas fireplace is more separate from the dining area, where space is allowed for a buffet. The master bedrooms in both units are served by ample closets and private baths.

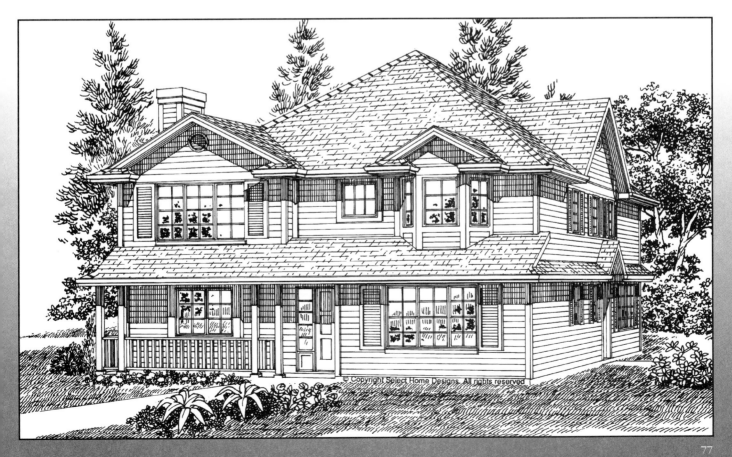

Plan HPT260075

Main Level: 586 sq. ft.
Lower Level: 586 sq. ft.
Total: 1,172 sq. ft. per unit

Width: 45'-0"
Depth: 28'-0"

Rhododendron Road

This simple yet traditional duplex design offers a comfortable and attractive family layout. Enter this split-level design to find easy access to the main and lower levels from the entry area. Upstairs, the main level features a U-shaped kitchen connecting to a powder bath, and a combined living and dining area. The lower level is reserved for the family sleeping quarters, which comfortably accommodate a master bedroom and two secondary bedrooms. All three family bedrooms share access to a full hall bath and a laundry closet.

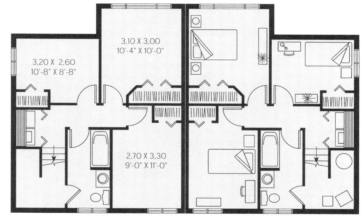

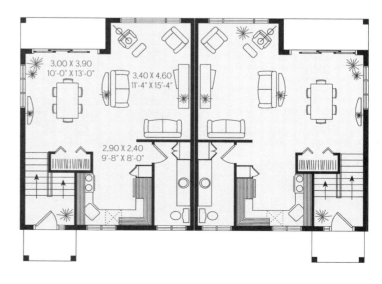

Oak Pointe

This contemporary duplex design provides two separate two-story units. The first floor of each unit offers a combined living and dining area. The kitchen and laundry/powder room are comfortably located at the rear of the plan. A stairway leads up to the family sleeping quarters, which includes a large master bedroom with a spacious walk-in closet and two smaller family bedrooms at the rear. All three bedrooms share a full hall bath that contains a soaking tub, a separate shower compartment, a toilet and a vanity sink. This home is designed with a basement foundation.

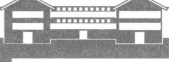

Plan HPT260076

First Floor: 586 sq. ft.
Second Floor: 616 sq. ft.
Total: 1,202 sq. ft. per unit

Width: 40'-0"
Depth: 29'-0"

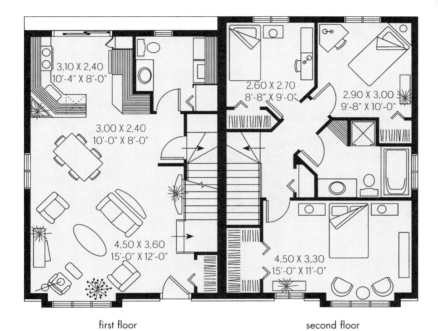

first floor

second floor

Plan HPT260077

Unit A
First Floor: 629 sq. ft.
Second Floor: 629 sq. ft.
Total: 1,258 sq. ft.
Unit B
First Floor: 629 sq. ft.
Second Floor: 654 sq. ft.
Total: 1,283 sq. ft.

Width: 46'-0"
Depth: 34'-0"

Tanager Drive

An attractive mix of vertical and horizontal siding, dormers and gables lends traditional appeal
to this American duplex home. Inside, two
floors of livability provide mirror-image floor
plans. The entry opens immediately inside to the
spacious living room. The U-shaped kitchen
connects to the dining area, which overlooks the
rear porch. A powder room and laundry closet
complete the first floor. Upstairs, two family
bedrooms share a full bath between them and a
hall linen closet. The master bedroom features a
large walk-in closet and a private balcony overlooking the backyard. Please specify crawlspace
or slab foundation when ordering.

Maple Ridge Road

Horizontal and vertical siding enclose two-story floor plans for each duplex. The interior plans provide mirror-image designs—one unit offers a petite front covered porch, while the other unit provides a larger front covered porch. Each unit enters directly into the combined living and dining area, which is warmed by a fireplace. The efficient compact kitchen is placed across from a utility room. A large rear patio is accessed nearby for outdoor entertaining. Upstairs, two family bedrooms share a full hall bath, and the master bedroom features a spacious closet. Please specify crawlspcae or slab foundation when ordering.

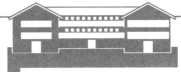

Plan HPT260078

First Floor: 478 sq. ft.
Second Floor: 478 sq. ft.
Total: 956 sq. ft. per unit

Width: 44'-0"
Depth: 31'-0"

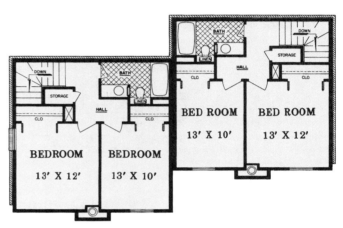

Plan HPT260079

Unit A
First Floor: 629 sq. ft.
Second Floor: 629 sq. ft.
Total: 1,258 sq. ft.
Unit B
First Floor: 629 sq. ft.
Second Floor: 654 sq. ft.
Total: 1,283 sq. ft.

Width: 46'-0"
Depth: 34'-0"

Korel Hollow

Stone and Tudor details lend an exquisite Elizabethan ambiance to this European-style duplex. Mirror-image floor plans are provided inside. The foyer opens to a living room that combines with the dining area for a larger entertainment space. A rear porch outside the dining room could be great for outdoor grilling. A laundry closet is placed across from the U-shaped kitchen. A powder room is located underneath the stairway. Upstairs, two family bedrooms share direct access to a full bath. The master suite features a walk-in closet and a private balcony. Please specify crawlspace or slab foundation when ordering.

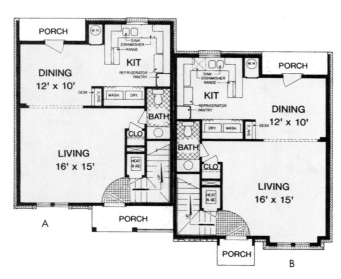

Nantucket Bay

With charming European accents, this dazzling duplex home offers style and comfortable livability. Mirror-image floor plans are offered inside, accessed from two first-floor entries. The foyer leads into a great room—ideal for casual or formal family gatherings. The island kitchen opens to a dining area. A powder room and a two-car garage complete the first floor. Upstairs, the master suite provides a private shower bath and walk-in closet. Bedrooms 2 and 3 share a full hall bath between them.

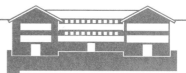

Plan HPT260080

First Floor: 709 sq. ft.
Second Floor: 801 sq. ft.
Total: 1,510 sq. ft. per unit

Width: 60'-0"
Depth: 42'-0"

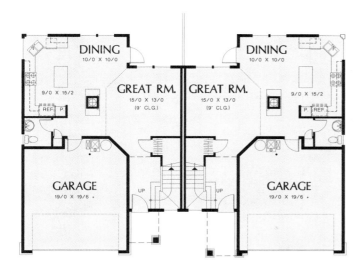

Plan HPT260081

First Floor: 647 sq. ft.
Second Floor: 647 sq. ft.
Total: 1,294 sq. ft. per unit

Width: 48'-0"
Depth: 32'-0"

Queens Village Square

A traditional silhouette encloses this practical two-story duplex home. A single front covered porch welcomes you inside to each apartment unit. The entryway introduces a powder room and hall closet. A hallway leads past the compact kitchen and laundry closet. The dining room opens to the living room, which is warmed by a fireplace. A porch and patio, accessed from the dining room, are perfect for outdoor grilling and seasonal entertainment. Upstairs, two bedrooms share a bath, but feature their own separate vanities. One bedroom offers two separate closets, while the additional bedroom provides a small walk-in closet. Please specify crawlspace or slab foundation when ordering.

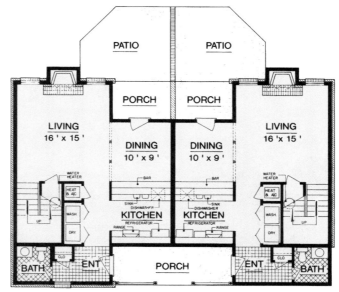

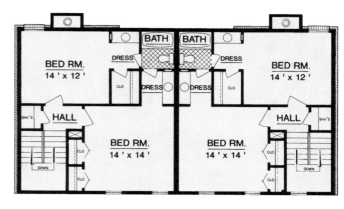

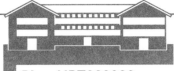

Plan HPT260082

First Floor: 647 sq. ft.
Second Floor: 647 sq. ft.
Total: 1,294 sq. ft. per unit

Width: 48'-0"
Depth: 32'-0"

Myrtle Beach Grove

Siding and shingled accents enclose a cozy two-story floor plan. A wide covered front porch welcomes you inside to an entryway that introduces a powder room. A laundry closet is located across from the kitchen. The dining room accesses a porch/patio— great for entertaining. The living room is warmed by a fireplace. Upstairs, two family bedrooms share a bath, but feature separate private vanities. One bedroom offers two closets, while the secondary bedroom provides a walk-in closet. Both bedrooms share a hall linen closet. Please specify crawlspace or slab foundation when ordering.

Plan HPT260083

First Floor: 785 sq. ft.
Second Floor: 902 sq. ft.
Total: 1,687 sq. ft. per unit

Width: 56'-0"
Depth: 56'-0"

Nutmeg Circle

With shingles, stonework, a trellis-covered front walk and twin gables, this fine two-story duplex is sure to please. Inside, the two-story living room greets friends and family alike, offering a fireplace and built-in media center for cozy get-togethers. The C-shaped kitchen features a window over the sink, plenty of counter and cabinet space, and a serving counter into the dining room. A laundry room and a half-bath complete this level. Upstairs, two secondary bedrooms—one with a walk-in closet—share a full hall bath. The master suite offers a large walk-in closet and a pampering private bath.

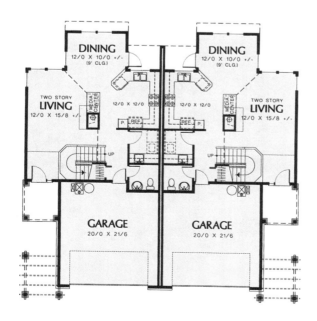

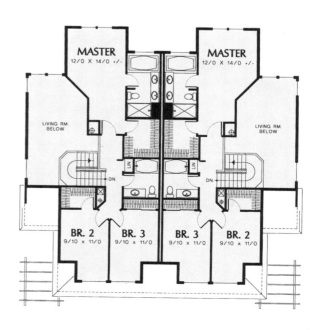

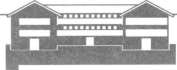

Ammar Place

Symmetry pervades this efficient and comfortable two-story duplex. Inside each unit, a two-story great room offers a warming fireplace for those cool winter evenings. The dining room provides easy access to the rear yard, as well as to the C-shaped kitchen. A powder room completes this level. Upstairs, the sleeping zone is made up of a walk-in linen closet, a master suite with a private bath, and two secondary bedrooms sharing a full hall bath that features a dual-bowl vanity.

Plan HPT260084

First Floor: 704 sq. ft.
Second Floor: 782 sq. ft.
Total: 1,486 sq. ft. per unit

Width: 56'-0"
Depth: 47'-0"

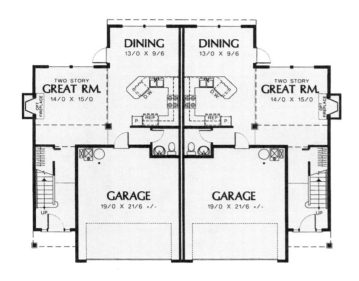

Plan HPT260085

First Floor: 620 sq. ft.
Second Floor: 832 sq. ft.
Total: 1,452 sq. ft. per unit

Width: 40'-0"
Depth: 52'-6"

Mt. Lemmon Drive

Two families fit nicely in this practical duplex plan in which each side is twenty-feet wide and a mirror image of the other. Enter the home through the foyer or the garage to the open dining room/living room combination. The angled counter of the adjacent kitchen overlooks the living room, which offers sliding glass doors to the outside. A powder room and two closets are also on the first floor. Upstairs, two family bedrooms share a hall bath. A linen closet and laundry facilities are also located on this floor.

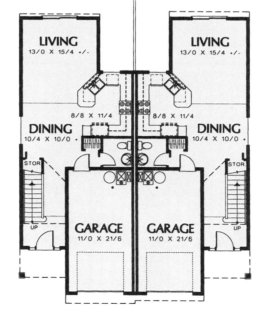

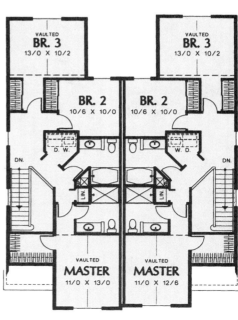

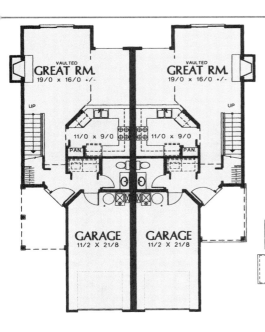

Plan HPT260086

First Floor: 596 sq. ft.
Second Floor: 601 sq. ft.
Total: 1,197 sq. ft. per unit

Width: 40'-0"
Depth: 53'-0"

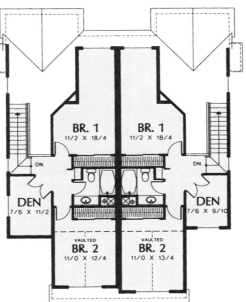

Southwood Lane

Petite yet cozy—with a vaulted great room warmed by a fireplace, a U-shaped kitchen with lots of counter and cabinet space, and an upstairs sleeping zone, this two-story duplex will fit almost any lifestyle. Sliding glass doors lead from the great room to the rear yard. Upstairs, the two bedrooms share a full bath, with the front bedroom featuring a vaulted ceiling. A cozy den finishes out this level, offering a perfect place for study, reading or a home office.

Plan HPT260087

Main Level: 1,050 sq. ft.
Lower Level: 528 sq. ft.
Total: 1,578 sq. ft. per unit

Width: 66'-0"
Depth: 39'-6"

Keaton's Pointe

Clean lines and many amenities make these two units worth a second look. The entry of each unit is split, providing two distinct upper and lower levels. Both of these lovely duplex units offer two bedrooms, an eat-in kitchen, a fireplace in the living room and a rear wood deck for stargazing—all conveniently placed on the main level, while a third bedroom, a full bath and a good-sized recreation room complete the lower level. The master bedroom enjoys a window seat overlooking the front yard and a walk-in closet. Both units offer a two-car garage.

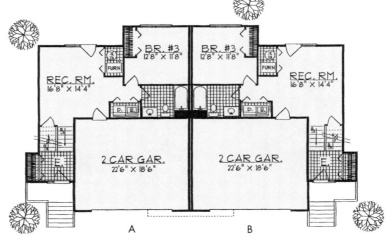

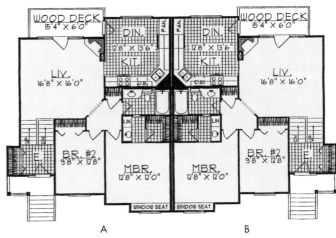

Catalina Bend

With the great room to the rear, there will be no street noise to ruin your gatherings! A covered stoop enters into a two-story foyer, where directly ahead, the great room is warmed by a fireplace. The U-shaped kitchen with efficient pantry space opens to a bayed breakfast room. A powder room and two-car garage complete the first floor. Upstairs, the master suite enjoys a large walk-in closet and a private bath. Bedrooms 2 and 3 share a full hall bath nearby. A laundry room is also located on the second floor for easy family convenience.

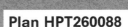

Plan HPT260088

First Floor: 829 sq. ft.
Second Floor: 989 sq. ft.
Total: 1,818 sq. ft. per unit

Width: 56'-0"
Depth: 54'-0"

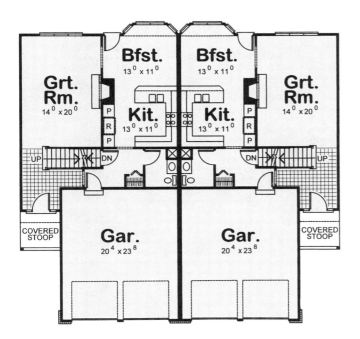

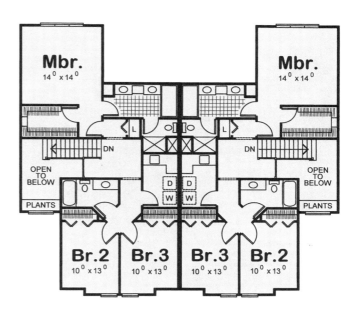

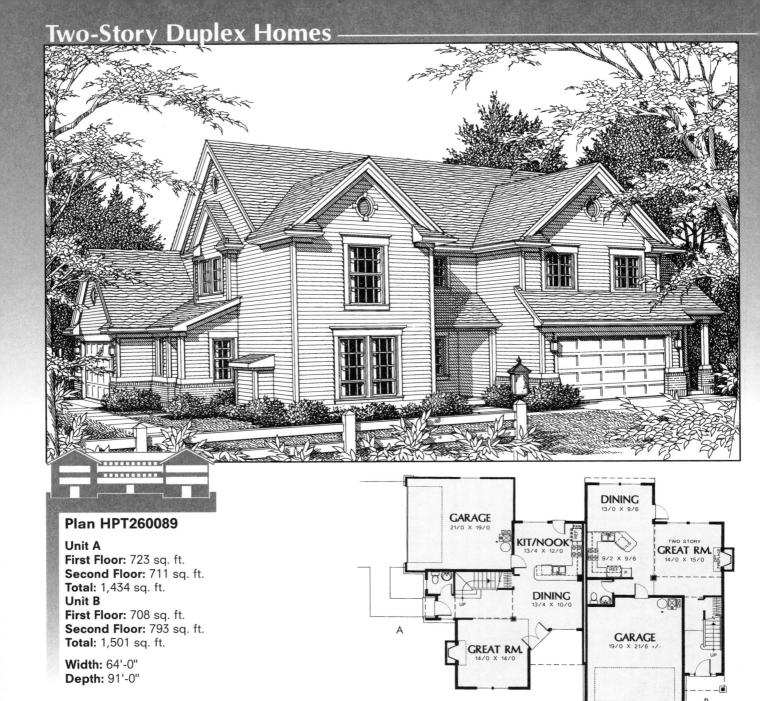

Plan HPT260089

Unit A
First Floor: 723 sq. ft.
Second Floor: 711 sq. ft.
Total: 1,434 sq. ft.
Unit B
First Floor: 708 sq. ft.
Second Floor: 793 sq. ft.
Total: 1,501 sq. ft.

Width: 64'-0"
Depth: 91'-0"

Rosewood Falls

This farmhouse design combines two separate floor plans under one roof—a perfect arrangement for relatives or tenants. Each residence provides a master suite, secondary bedrooms, a formal dining room, a great room and its own garage. The left plan offers a centered fireplace in the great room and lovely views of the front property, while the second plan's great room looks to the backyard. Each plan enjoys a well-organized kitchen, which serves both a dining room and a snack bar or nook. The second floor of the right plan features a balcony hall overlooking the great room.

Hazelton Avenue

Four gables, a siding-and-brick facade and columns framing a covered porch all combine to give this fine duplex plenty of curb appeal. Inside, a two-story foyer leads to the great room, where a through-fireplace is shared with the efficient U-shaped kitchen. The nearby dining area offers access to the rear yard. Upstairs, two secondary bedrooms share a full bath that includes a dual-bowl vanity, while the master bedroom suite features a walk-in closet and a private bath. A laundry room finishes out this level. The two-car garage will easily shelter the family fleet.

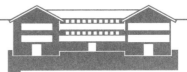

Plan HPT260090

First Floor: 655 sq. ft.
Second Floor: 809 sq. ft.
Total: 1,464 sq. ft. per unit

Width: 60'-0"
Depth: 42'-0"

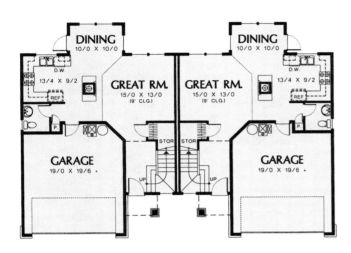

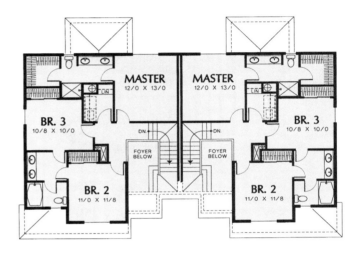

Plan HPT262015

First Floor: 801 sq. ft.
Second Floor: 900 sq. ft.
Total: 1,701 sq. ft. per unit

Width: 56'-0"
Depth: 56'-0"

Villa Cherie

With shingles, stonework, a trellis-covered front walk and twin gables, this fine two-story duplex is sure to please. Inside, the two-story living room greets friends and family alike, offering a fireplace and built-in media center for cozy get-togethers. The C-shaped kitchen features a window over the sink, plenty of counter and cabinet space, and a serving counter into the dining room. A laundry room and a half-bath complete this level. Upstairs, two secondary bedrooms—one with a walk-in closet—share a full hall bath. The master suite offers a large walk-in closet and a pampering private bath.

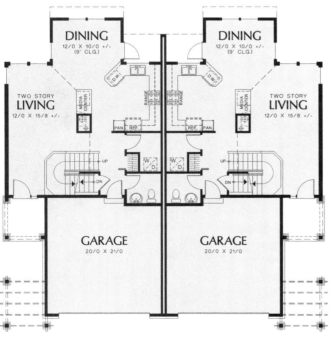

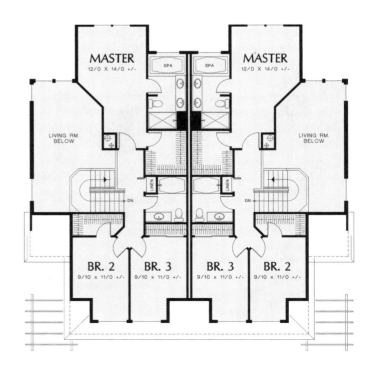

Twilight Corner

This stately bayed beauty is home to two comfortable units with slightly different layouts. The first-floor unit has a little extra closet space and an angled bath. Upstairs, washer-and-dryer space and a small additional room at the top of the stairs make the difference. Both units have two bedrooms flanking a hall bath and a generously sized living and dining area that looks out from a bay window and flows into a roomy kitchen. A leisurely balcony or patio complements each plan. This home is designed with a basement foundation.

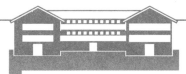

Plan HPT262016

First-floor Unit: 987 sq. ft.
Second-floor Unit: 1,016 sq. ft.

Width: 33'-4"
Depth: 37'-8"

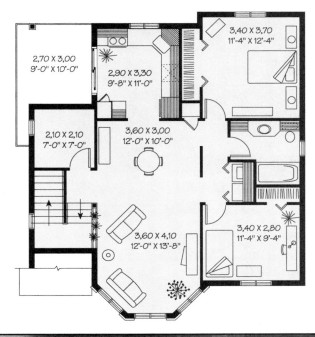

Plan HPT262017

Unit A
First Floor: 787 sq. ft.
Second Floor: 788 sq. ft.
Total: 1,575 sq. ft.
Bonus Space: 353 sq. ft.
Unit B
First Floor: 853 sq. ft.
Second Floor: 796 sq. ft.
Total: 1,649 sq. ft.

Width: 80'-0"
Depth: 48'-0"

Cassady Wood

Each of these duplex homes has its own distinct personality! The unit on the left is accented with dormers and gables, while the right is more simple, yet just as attractive. Both units open into spacious family rooms and each features a utility room, first-floor powder room and a two-car garage. The left unit's island kitchen works with a breakfast area to create space for dining, while upstairs, three bedrooms, including a large master suite, reside. A special feature here is the 353 square feet of extra storage space. The unit on the right features a dining room between the kitchen and family room. Its second floor is home to three bedrooms and two baths.

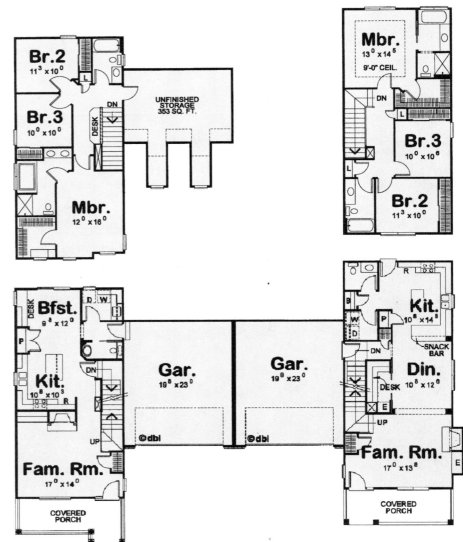

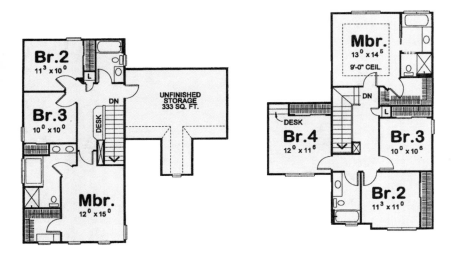

Plan HPT262018

Unit A
First Floor: 787 sq. ft.
Second Floor: 773 sq. ft.
Total: 1,560 sq. ft.
Bonus Space: 353 sq. ft.
Unit B
First Floor: 896 sq. ft.
Second Floor: 1,005 sq. ft.
Total: 1,901 sq. ft.

Width: 80'-0"
Depth: 46'-0"

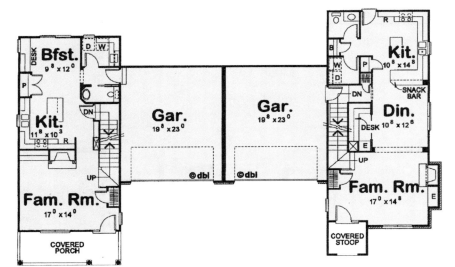

Taffeta Minuet

With its two different facades, this Craftsman-style duplex creates the illusion of two separate homes. Each unit opens into an enormous family room, warmed by a fireplace. Unit A on the left features an island kitchen flowing into a breakfast area. A roomy pantry sits between the two spaces, right across from the garage entry and the utility room. Upstairs, 353 square feet of storage space resides along with three bedrooms. The master suite has a walk-in closet and a spacious private bath. Unit B's family room flows into a dining area, which leads to the U-shaped island kitchen. Four bedrooms, including a luxurious master suite, reside on the second floor. Both units are equipped with two baths and a powder room, as well as a two-car garage.

Plan HPT260095

Unit A
First Floor: 838 sq. ft.
Second Floor: 390 sq. ft.
Total: 1,228 sq. ft.
Unit B
First Floor: 600 sq. ft.
Second Floor: 501 sq. ft.
Total: 1,101 sq. ft.

Width: 80'-7"
Depth: 37'-10"

Yorktown Bay

This contemporary duplex design features two two-story units with slightly altered floor plans. Unit A features a living room/dining area that connects to a compact kitchen located at the rear of the plan. A patio is provided for outdoor grilling. The first-floor master bedroom features a private bath and walk-in closet. The first floor is completed by a two-car garage. Two additional family bedrooms are located on the second floor of Unit A, along with a hall bath. Unit B includes a living room, kitchen, dining area, outdoor patio and two-garage on the first floor, while two family bedrooms—including the master suite reside on the second floor.

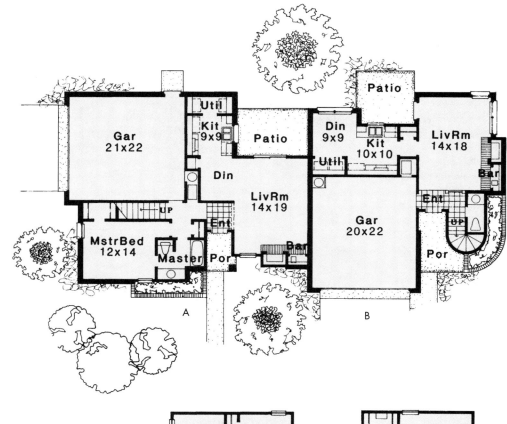

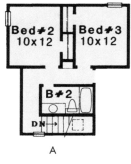

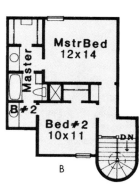

Inspiration Pointe

Contemporary and cozy for any young family, this stylish duplex design offers two comfortable floors of livability. Unit A enters from a front porch into a two-story entry foyer. The living room, warmed by a fireplace, overlooks the rear patio. The kitchen opens to a dining area. The second bedroom is tucked away at the rear of the plan and uses the full hall bath. A utility room and single-car garage complete the first floor. Unit B offers the same rooms in its first-floor layout, but includes an additional third bedroom. The second floor of each plan provides a private master bedroom complete with a master bath and walk-in closet.

Plan HPT260096

Unit A
First Floor: 1,174 sq. ft.
Second Floor: 388 sq. ft.
Total: 1,562 sq. ft.
Unit B
First Floor: 1,274 sq. ft.
Second Floor: 388 sq. ft.
Total: 1,662 sq. ft.

Width: 102'-4"
Depth: 47'-1"

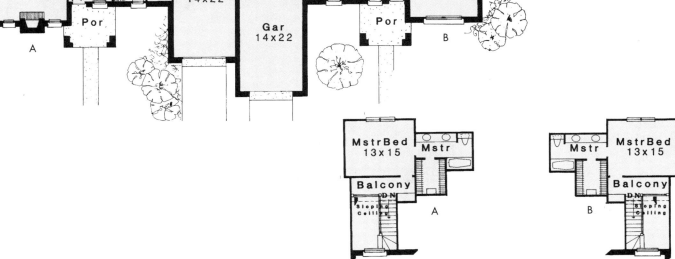

Plan HPT262019

First Floor: 896 sq. ft.
Second Floor: 1,005 sq. ft.
Total: 1,901 sq. ft. per unit

Width: 80'-0"
Depth: 49'-4"

Scarlet Pony Way

This two-story duplex features mirror-image floor plans. Enter the hearth-warmed family room from a covered stoop. Straight ahead lies the dining area—with its unique built-in desk space, it doubles as a study between mealtimes. At the back of the plan, the spacious island kitchen features loads of counter space and a roomy pantry. A utility room and a half-bath complete the first floor. Upstairs, three family bedrooms, all with plenty of closet space, are across the hall from the tray-ceilinged master suite, which delights with a private bath. Bedrooms 2 and 4 are equipped with built-in desks.

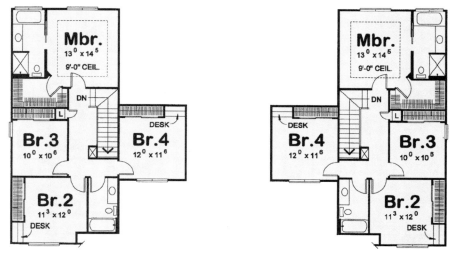

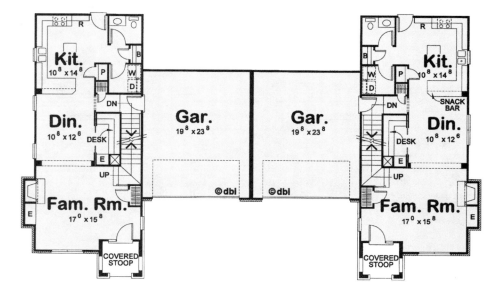

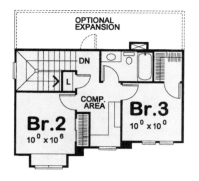

OPTIONAL EXPANSION

DN

COMP. AREA

Br.2
10⁰ x 10⁶

Br.3
10⁰ x 10⁰

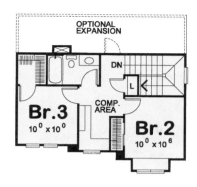

OPTIONAL EXPANSION

DN

COMP. AREA

Br.3
10⁰ x 10⁰

Br.2
10⁰ x 10⁶

Plan HPT262020

First Floor: 1,268 sq. ft.
Second Floor: 431 sq. ft.
Total: 1,699 sq. ft. per unit

Width: 80'-0"
Depth: 47'-8"

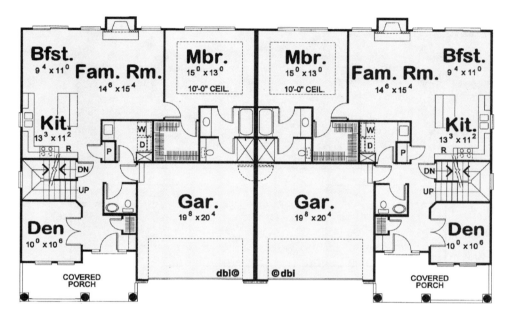

Bfst.
9⁴ x 11⁰

Fam. Rm.
14⁶ x 15⁴

Mbr.
15⁰ x 13⁰
10'-0" CEIL.

Mbr.
15⁰ x 13⁰
10'-0" CEIL.

Fam. Rm.
14⁶ x 15⁴

Bfst.
9⁴ x 11⁰

Kit.
13³ x 11²

W
D
P

W
D
P

Kit.
13³ x 11²

DN
UP

DN
UP

Gar.
19⁸ x 20⁴

Gar.
19⁸ x 20⁴

Den
10⁰ x 10⁶

COVERED PORCH

dbl©

©dbl

COVERED PORCH

Den
10⁰ x 10⁶

Tiara Grande

Who says a duplex has to be limited? These floor plans have all the extras—starting with a den and a first-floor master suite. Enter into a foyer complete with a coat closet. From here, double doors open to a cozy den. Straight ahead, the garage entry is flanked by a convenient half-bath and the utility room. In back, the island kitchen flows gracefully into the breakfast nook and family room. The family room's fireplace will warm you up whether you're preparing meals, dining, or just relaxing. The master bedroom, with its roomy walk-in closet and lush private bath, completes the first floor. Upstairs, two bedrooms—one with a walk-in closet—share a bath and a handy built-in computer area.

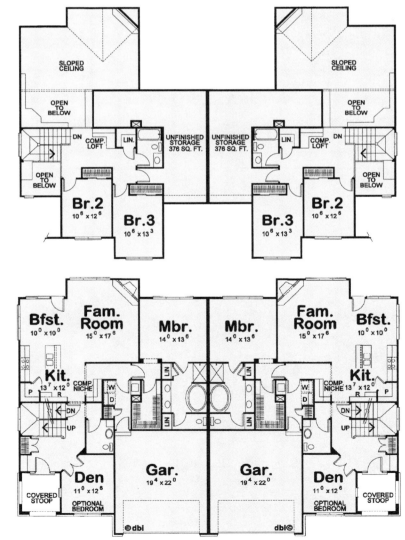

Plan HPT262021

First Floor: 1,497 sq. ft.
Second Floor: 554 sq. ft.
Total: 2,051 sq. ft. per unit
Bonus Space: 376 sq. ft. per unit

Width: 80'-0"
Depth: 55'-0"

Tosca's Delight

The elegant stucco facade and sloping wing rooflines give this duplex the look of a swanky estate! Shutters and stone accents add more stylish touches. Inside, the floor plans mirror each other. Step into a gallery hallway that opens to a den and faces the staircase. The island kitchen opens out to the breakfast nook and family room. A corner fireplace warms these areas. The first-floor master suite is separated from the living areas by a long hallway. Upstairs, two bedrooms and a bath are complemented by 376 square feet of bonus space and a handy computer loft.

Ivy Terrace

Though it looks like a single-family home on the outside, this plan actually houses two units—a compact one-story apartment and a family-size two-story. Unit A on the right opens into a spacious living/dining area that leads back to the L-shaped kitchen. To the left is a convenient half-bath/utility room. Upstairs, three bedrooms, including a spacious master bedroom with a huge wall-length closet, share a deluxe bath. Unit B on the left keeps it all together downstairs, with many of the same amenities: an L-shaped kitchen, utility room, and roomy bedroom closet. The bedroom features double doors out to the rear property. This home is designed with a basement foundation.

Plan HPT262022

Unit A
First Floor: 685 sq. ft.
Second Floor: 874 sq. ft.
Total: 1,559 sq. ft.
Unit B
Square Footage: 619

Width: 37'-0"
Depth: 38'-0"

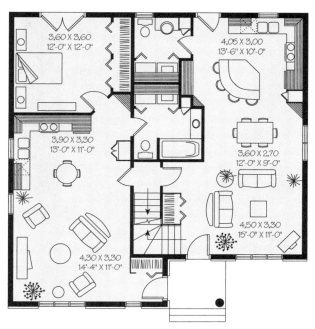

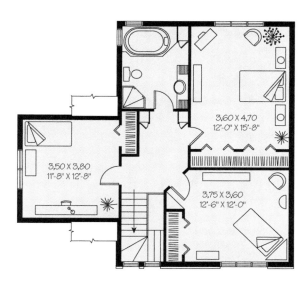

Plan HPT262023

Square Footage: 972 per unit

Width: 32'-0"
Depth: 34'-0"

Cymbeline Court

This trim two-story duplex makes good use of its space with a unit on each floor. Each begins with a sizable living/dining area that leads to an L-shaped kitchen. The second-floor's kitchen has a door to a petite balcony, while the first floor leads to a small patio. The left side of both units is taken up by two bedrooms—one could easily be converted to a den—and a hall bath. Washer-and-dryer space and three closets apiece finish off these units nicely. This home is designed with a basement foundation.

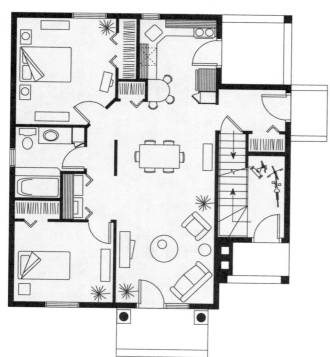

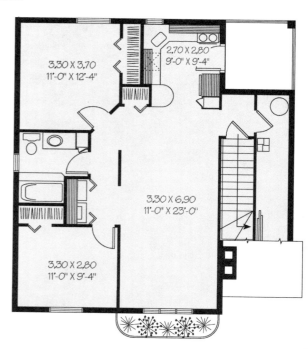

Plan HPT260102

Units A + AR
First Floor: 554 sq. ft.
Second Floor: 460 sq. ft.
Total: 1,014 sq. ft.
Unit B
Square Footage: 936

Width: 46'-10"
Depth: 66'-2"

Muth's Mill

This unique northwestern contemporary design features three separate apartment units. Units A and AR offer two floors of livability. The first floors provide a living room with a fireplace, a kitchen/dining area and an outdoor patio. Upstairs, the master bedroom and Bedroom 2 each have a walk-in closet and share a bath. Unit B is a one-story apartment, which enters from an outdoor porch directly into the living room, warmed by a fireplace. A utility room is placed near the kitchen/dining area. The master bedroom features a walk-in closet and a private half-bath, while Bedroom 2 is placed on the opposite side of the full hall bath.

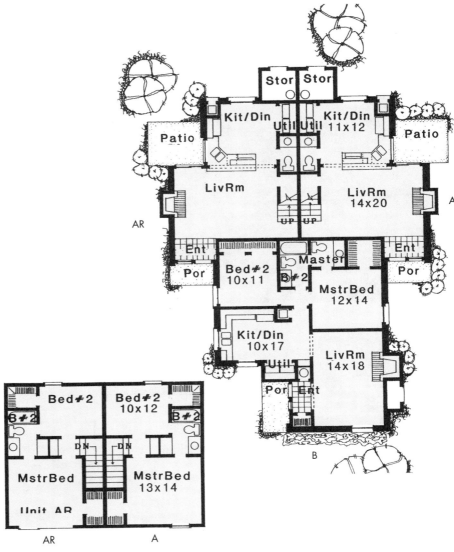

Plan HPT260103

Units A + C
Square Footage: 1,376
Finished Basement:
582 sq. ft.
Unit B
First Floor: 1,707 sq. ft.
Second Floor: 527 sq. ft.
Total: 2,234 sq. ft.
Finished Basement: 832

Width: 92'-0"
Depth: 72'-0

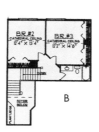

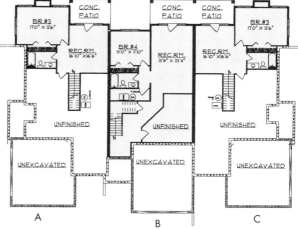

Manhattan Circle

This impressive multiplex design features three separate units with some slight variations. Units A and C provide mirror-image layouts of each other. These layouts include a two-car garage, a den connecting to a hall bath, a laundry room, U-shaped kitchen, dining room, great room warmed by a fireplace, master bedroom with a private bath and walk-in closet, and a rear wood deck for the first-floor design. The finished basement design features a recreation room, third bedroom, a third bath, a covered patio and unfinished space for storage. Unit B offers a similar first-floor layout, but features stairs leading to the second floor. Two additional bedrooms are located on this second floor, along with a hall bath. The basement level of Unit B provides an additional fourth bedroom.

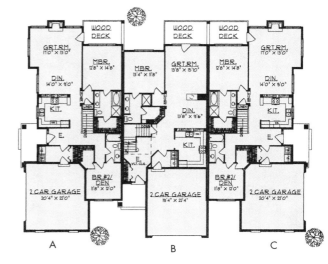

Isabella Park

This compact and efficient triplex plan features three units with well-appointed layouts. Enter inside each unit, where a study and two-car garage flank the foyer. The study can be converted to a second bedroom—perfect for a nursery or guest room. A full hall bath is located nearby for convenience. The combined great room/dining area is vaulted to create a better sense of spaciousness and is warmed by a fireplace. This area accesses the rear screened porch, placed next to the wood deck. The kitchen opens to a breakfast nook. A laundry closet is located nearby. The master bedroom is a private haven with its own bath and walk-in closet/dressing room.

Plan HPT260104

Square Footage:
1,428 per unit

Width: 121'-0"
Depth: 55'-8"

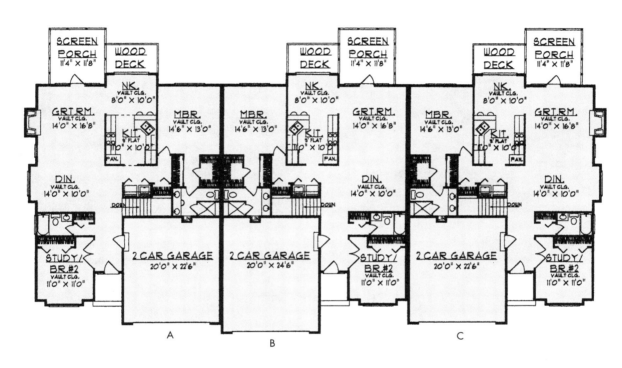

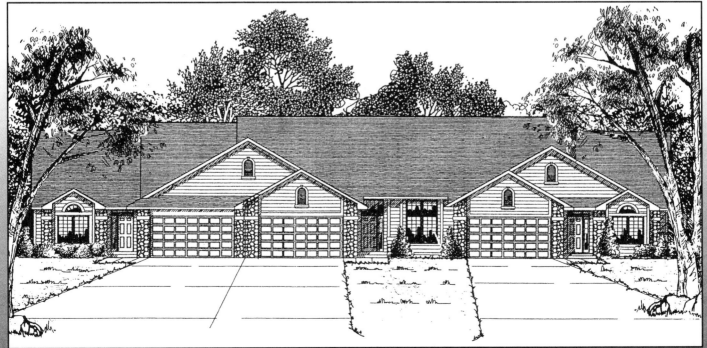

Plan HPT260105

Square Footage: 912 per unit

Width: 48'-0"
Depth: 38'-0"

Concord Square

This traditional four-plex home possesses a distinct New England flavor—perfect for new families just starting out. An entry porch welcomes you inside to a family room. The island countertop kitchen opens to a breakfast room. A grilling porch is featured at the rear of the unit and offers an outdoor storage closet for seasonal supplies. Each unit offers two bedrooms—the master bedroom is slightly larger and provides more closet space. Both family bedrooms share the full hall bath that includes the laundry closet.

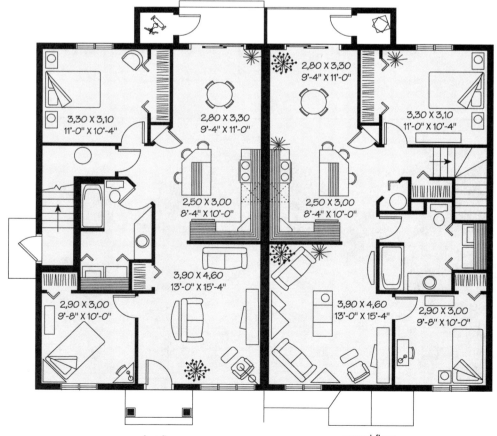

3,30 X 3,10
11'-0" X 10'-4"

2,80 X 3,30
9'-4" X 11'-0"

2,80 X 3,30
9'-4" X 11'-0"

3,30 X 3,10
11'-0" X 10'-4"

2,50 X 3,00
8'-4" X 10'-0"

2,50 X 3,00
8'-4" X 10'-0"

3,90 X 4,60
13'-0" X 15'-4"

3,90 X 4,60
13'-0" X 15'-4"

2,90 X 3,00
9'-8" X 10'-0"

2,90 X 3,00
9'-8" X 10'-0"

first floor

second floor

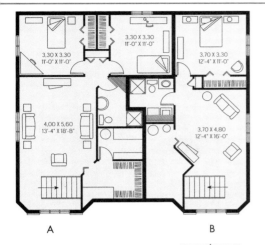

A   B

A   B

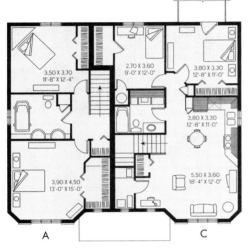

A   C

Plan HPT260106

Unit A
Main Level: 599 sq. ft.
Upper Level: 669 sq. ft.
Lower Level: 906 sq. ft
Total: 2,174 sq. ft.
Unit B
Main Level: 755 sq. ft.
Lower Level: 652 sq. ft.
Total: 1,407 sq. ft.
Unit C
Square Footage: 884 sq. ft.

Width: 42'-0"
Depth: 38'-0"

Orchard Bend

Three separate units are housed in this townhome, each with a covered front entrance. Unit A occupies three floors, with the kitchen, dining room, breakfast nook and laundry facilities on the first floor. A short flight of stairs off of the entry leads to the lower level where a living room, full bath and two bedrooms are located. The third floor contains a full bath and two additional bedrooms. Unit B includes an eat-in kitchen, living room, bedroom and full bath on the first level. A family room, full bath and additional bedroom can be found on the lower level. Access unit C via a flight of stairs to the second level, where a living room, eat-in kitchen and two bedrooms are featured. This home is designed with a basement foundation.

Plan HPT260107

Unit A
First Floor: 607 sq. ft.
Second Floor: 694 sq. ft.
Total: 1,301 sq. ft.
Unit B
First Floor: 716 sq. ft.
Second Floor: 761 sq. ft.
Total: 1,477 sq. ft.
Unit C
First Floor: 763 sq. ft.
Second Floor: 748 sq. ft.
Total: 1,511 sq. ft.

Width: 67'-8"
Depth: 38'-4"

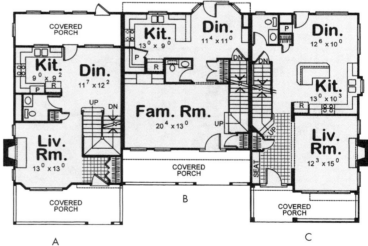

Merrill Park

A traditional silhouette outlines the exterior of this multi-family unit, while efficient layouts are provided within. Each unit provides a slightly altered floor plan. Regardless of shape or size, each unit offers a front covered porch that enters inside. Each end unit provides an entry and living room warmed by a fireplace, while the middle unit opens to a spacious family room. A kitchen opening to a breakfast room and a powder room complete the first floor of each unit—one unit offers a rear covered porch. The second floor of each apartment consists of a master bedroom with a private bath and walk-in closet and two additional bedrooms that share a hall bath.

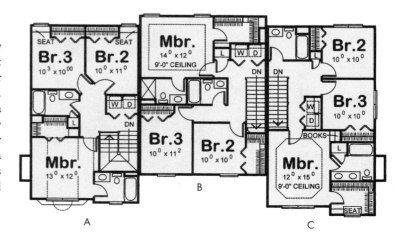

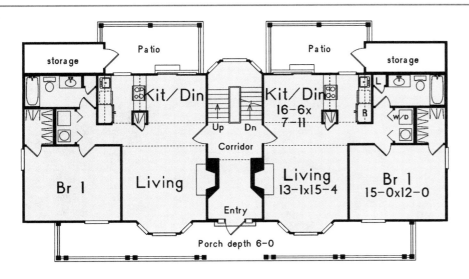

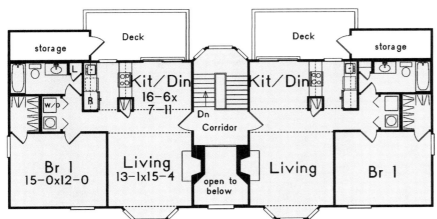

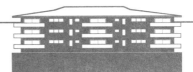

Plan HPT260108

Square Footage: 710 per unit

Width: 66'-6"
Depth: 38'-0"

Virginia Circle

This multi-family option provides traditional apartment living for quiet empty-nesters. The exterior is dazzled with old-fashioned American charm, while the interior units provide efficient living. Each of the four units enjoys a cozy living room warmed by a fireplace and brightened by a bay window. The kitchen space overlooks the dining area, opening to the rear. The bedroom features a walk-in closet, just across from the full hall bath. The downstairs units enjoy front covered-porch access and rear patios with storage rooms. The upstairs units feature second-floor rear decks, also with storage—perfect for outdoor grilling.

Plan HPT260109

Square Footage:
1,060 per unit

Width: 80'-0"
Depth: 51'-8"

Sarasota Grove

With stylish European and Mediterranean accents, this dazzling Old World design provides a stunning multi-family option for the growing family. A quaint front covered porch welcomes you inside to a two-story foyer, overlooked by a second-floor balcony. Each of the four units provides nearly identical layouts. The living room enjoys a charming corner fireplace, across from the bayed kitchen area. Bedrooms 2 and 3 share a full hall bath, while the master bedroom includes a walk-in closet and private bath. Each unit provides a laundry closet, equipped for a washer and dryer. The first-floor units offer rear patios, while the second-floor units offer rear decks.

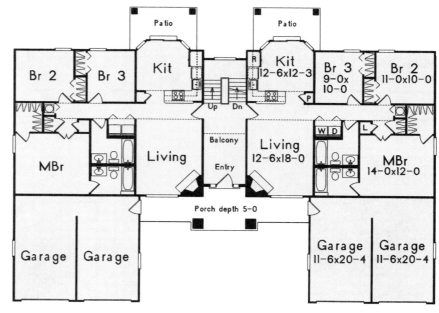

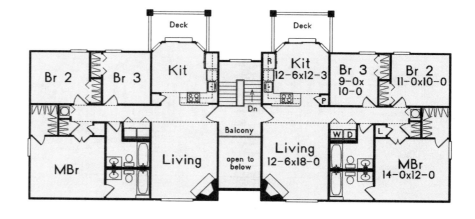

Abbington Place

Perfect for the California coast, this multi-family option provides multiple levels of living. The outer unit features a main-level floor plan that includes a kitchen with a pantry, a combined living/dining space warmed by a fireplace, a master bedroom with a private whirlpool-tub bath and a second bedroom located near a hall bath. A rear deck and a garage complete the main level, while stairs lead down to a lower level that features a third bedroom, a family room and future space. Enter the inner unit by a small front porch or the garage. The formal dining room opens to the living space, while the kitchen connects to both a nook and laundry room. The upper level of this unit features three family bedrooms.

Plan HPT260110

Unit A
Main Level: 1,149 sq. ft.
Upper Level: 558 sq. ft.
Total: 1,707 sq. ft.
Unit B
Main Level: 1,055 sq. ft.
Upper Level: 924 sq. ft.
Total: 1,979 sq. ft.

Width: 116'-0"
Depth: 72'-6"

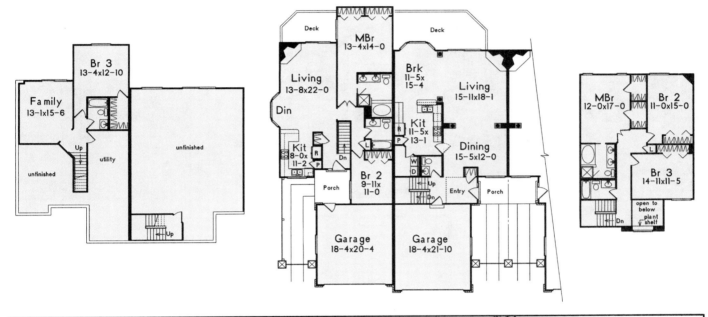

Plan HPT260111

Unit A
Square Footage: 630
Unit B
Main Level: 1,180 sq. ft.
Upper Level: 550 sq. ft.
Total: 1,730 sq. ft.
Unit C
Square Footage: 1,180

Width: 34'-0"
Depth: 37'-6"

Rosedale Park

This multi-family home boasts comfortable living space for the young family. Three floors, three units, each offering slightly different floor plans, all enclosed by a traditional brick and siding exterior. Each unit provides two family bedrooms, a living room and a kitchen. The main level features front-door access, a side carport, an enlarged master suite with a walk-in closet, a snack bar overlooking the dining area, a hall bath and a laundry closet. The upstairs unit is almost exactly identical, with a slightly altered bathroom layout. The basement-level unit features a game room, laundry room/hall bath, half-bath and a kitchen area opening to a combined living space. This home is designed with a basement foundation.

Peacock Park

This unique triplex home offers two two-story units and a finished basement-level apartment. The two-story apartments have mirror-image floor plans. The first floors of these units provide an open living/dining area and a kitchen with a snack bar. A powder room, a hall closet and pantry space complete this level. The second floors include two family bedrooms each, which share a hall bath and a convenient laundry room. The basement level offers a one-story apartment that includes living and dining space, a U-shaped kitchen, a laundry closet and two family bedrooms sharing a hall bath. Storage space is also provided at this level for all three apartments. This home is designed with a basement foundation.

Plan HPT260112

Unit A
Square Footage: 953 sq. ft.
Units B + C
First Floor: 608 sq. ft.
Second Floor: 612 sq. ft.
Total: 1,220 sq. ft. per unit

Width: 36'-0"
Depth: 34'-0"

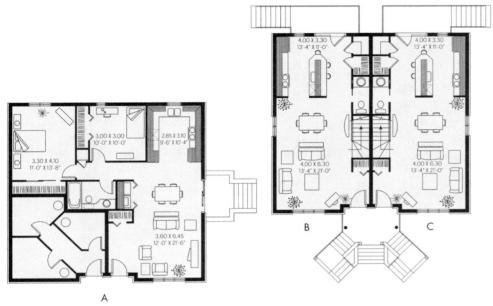

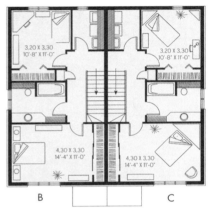

Huntington Plaza

This eight-unit structure features a brick exterior design. Each unit enters inside from a wide side porch shared with a neighboring apartment. The dining area combines with the living room for a spacious entertainment area. This area is warmed by a corner fireplace. The efficient compact kitchen is central to the unit. This design is perfect for empty-nesters or retired couples—a single large bedroom features His and Hers walk-in closets, a dressing area and direct access to the full hall bath. A laundry closet is located nearby.

Plan HPT260113

Square Footage: 868 per unit

Width: 88'-0"
Depth: 48'-0"

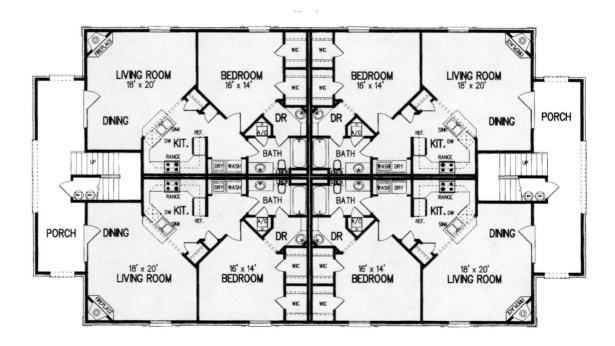

Ramsey Heights

This multiplex design has eight apartment units with features for young families. The first-floor units offer an outdoor porch, while the second-floor apartments provide balconies. Each unit enters into the living room, complete with a warming fireplace. A U-shaped kitchen opens to a dining area—a laundry closet is located nearby. The master suite features a private bath and walk-in closet. The secondary bedroom directly accesses a hall bath and features a walk-in closet as well. Linen storage is available nearby.

Plan HPT260114

Square Footage:
1,218 per unit

Width: 76'-0"
Depth: 92'-0"

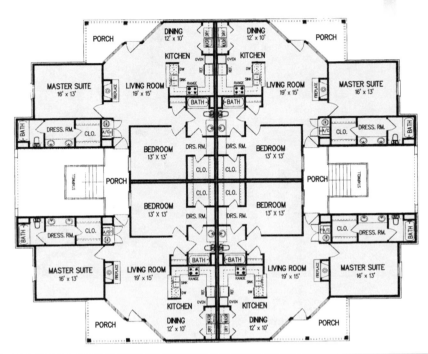

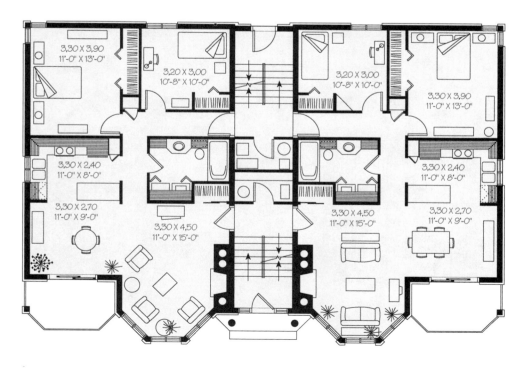

Plan HPT260115

Square Footage: 948 per unit

Width: 58'-0"
Depth: 40'-0"

Primrose Pointe

This elegant apartment building, dazzled in European and Victorian accents, features eight mirror-image interior layouts throughout. Each apartment unit offers a window bay at the front, which illuminates the formal living areas. The living room provides a warming fireplace and the open dining area is located nearby. The efficient island countertop kitchen serves these formal areas with ease. The master bedroom and secondary bedroom—each with a wall closet—share a full hall bath, located across from the kitchen. Here, a laundry closet provides space for a washer and dryer. This home is designed with a basement foundation.

LET US SHOW YOU OUR HOME BLUEPRINT PACKAGE.

BUILDING A HOME? PLANNING A HOME?

OUR BLUEPRINT PACKAGE HAS NEARLY EVERYTHING YOU NEED TO GET THE JOB DONE RIGHT,

whether you're working on your own or with help from an architect, designer, builder or subcontractors. Each Blueprint Package is the result of many hours of work by licensed architects or professional designers.

QUALITY

Hundreds of hours of painstaking effort have gone into the development of your blueprint plan. Each home has been quality-checked by professionals to insure accuracy and buildability.

VALUE

Because we sell in volume, you can buy professional quality blueprints at a fraction of their development cost. With our plans, your dream home design costs substantially less than the fees charged by architects.

SERVICE

Once you've chosen your favorite home plan, you'll receive fast, efficient service whether you choose to mail or fax your order to us or call us toll free at 1-800-521-6797. After you have received your order, call for customer service toll free 1-888-690-1116.

SATISFACTION

Over 50 years of service to satisfied home plan buyers provide us unparalleled experience and knowledge in producing quality blueprints.

ORDER TOLL FREE 1-800-521-6797

After you've looked over our Blueprint Package and Important Extras, call toll free on our Blueprint Hotline: 1-800-521-6797, for current pricing and availability prior to mailing the order form on page 125. We're ready and eager to serve you. After you have received your order, call for customer service toll free 1-888-690-1116.

Each set of blueprints is an interrelated collection of detail sheets which includes components such as floor plans, interior and exterior elevations, dimensions, cross-sections, diagrams and notations. These sheets show exactly how your house is to be built.

SETS MAY INCLUDE:

FRONTAL SHEET
This artist's sketch of the exterior of the house gives you an idea of how the house will look when built and landscaped. Large floor plans show all levels of the house and provide an overview of your new home's livability, as well as a handy reference for deciding on furniture placement.

FOUNDATION PLANS
This sheet shows the foundation layout including support walls, excavated and unexcavated areas, if any, and foundation notes. If slab construction rather than basement, the plan shows footings and details for a monolithic slab. This page, or another in the set, may include a sample plot plan for locating your house on a building site.

DETAILED FLOOR PLANS
These plans show the layout of each floor of the house. Rooms and interior spaces are carefully dimensioned and keys are given for cross-section details provided later in the plans. The positions of electrical outlets and switches are shown.

HOUSE CROSS-SECTIONS
Large-scale views show sections or cut-aways of the foundation, interior walls, exterior walls, floors, stairways and roof details. Additional cross-sections may show important changes in floor, ceiling or roof heights or the relationship of one level to another. Extremely valuable for construction, these sections show exactly how the various parts of the house fit together.

INTERIOR ELEVATIONS
Many of our drawings show the design and placement of kitchen and bathroom cabinets, laundry areas, fireplaces, bookcases and other built-ins. Little "extras," such as mantelpiece and wainscoting drawings, plus molding sections, provide details that give your home that custom touch.

EXTERIOR ELEVATIONS
These drawings show the front, rear and sides of your house and give necessary notes on exterior materials and finishes. Particular attention is given to cornice detail, brick and stone accents or other finish items that make your home unique.

INTRODUCING IMPORTANT PLANNING AND CONSTRUCTION
AIDS DEVELOPED BY OUR PROFESSIONALS TO HELP YOU
SUCCEED IN YOUR HOME-BUILDING PROJECT

MATERIALS LIST

(Note: Because of the diversity of local building codes, our Materials List does not include mechanical materials.)

For many of the designs in our portfolio, we offer a customized materials take-off that is invaluable in planning and estimating the cost of your new home. This Materials List outlines the quantity, type and size of materials needed to build your house (with the exception of mechanical system items). Included are framing lumber, windows and doors, kitchen and bath cabinetry, rough and finish hardware, and much more. This handy list helps you or your builder cost out materials and serves as a reference sheet when you're compiling bids. Some Materials Lists may be ordered before blueprints are ordered, call for information.

SPECIFICATION OUTLINE

This valuable 16-page document is critical to building your house correctly. Designed to be filled in by you or your builder, this book lists 166 stages or items crucial to the building process. It provides a comprehensive review of the construction process and helps in choosing materials. When combined with the blueprints, a signed contract, and a schedule, it becomes a legal document and record for the building of your home.

QUOTE ONE®

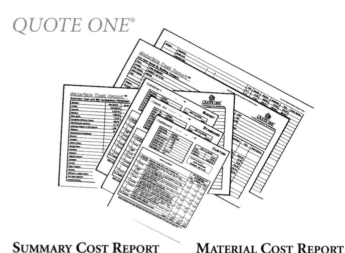

SUMMARY COST REPORT   **MATERIAL COST REPORT**

A product for estimating the cost of building select designs, the Quote One® system is available in two separate stages: The Summary Cost Report and the Material Cost Report.

The **Summary Cost Report** is the first stage in the package and shows the total cost per square foot for your chosen home in your zip-code area and then breaks that cost down into various categories showing the costs for building materials, labor and installation. The report includes three grades: Budget, Standard and Custom. These reports allow you to evaluate your building budget and compare the costs of building a variety of homes in your area.

Make even more informed decisions about your home-building project with the second phase of our package, our **Material Cost Report.** This tool is invaluable in planning and estimating the cost of your new home. The material and installation (labor and equipment) cost is shown for each of over 1,000 line items provided in the Materials List (Standard grade), which is included when you purchase this estimating tool. It allows you to determine building costs for your specific zip-code area and for your chosen home design. Space is allowed for additional estimates from contractors and subcontractors, such as for mechanical materials, which are not included in our packages. This invaluable tool includes a Materials List. A Material Cost Report cannot be ordered before blueprints are ordered. Call for details. In addition, ask about our Home Planners Estimating Package.

If you are interested in a plan that is not indicated as Quote One®, please call and ask our sales reps. They will be happy to verify the status for you. To order these invaluable reports, use the order form.

CONSTRUCTION INFORMATION

IF YOU WANT TO KNOW MORE ABOUT TECHNIQUES— and deal more confidently with subcontractors — we offer these useful sheets. Each set is an excellent tool that will add to your understanding of these technical subjects. These helpful details provide general construction information and are not specific to any single plan.

PLUMBING

The Blueprint Package includes locations for all the plumbing fixtures, including sinks, lavatories, tubs, showers, toilets, laundry trays and water heaters. However, if you want to know more about the complete plumbing system, these Plumbing Details will prove very useful. Prepared to meet requirements of the National Plumbing Code, these fact-filled sheets give general information on pipe schedules, fittings, sump-pump details, water-softener hookups, septic system details and much more. Sheets also include a glossary of terms.

ELECTRICAL

The locations for every electrical switch, plug and outlet are shown in your Blueprint Package. However, these Electrical Details go further to take the mystery out of household electrical systems. Prepared to meet requirements of the National Electrical Code, these comprehensive drawings come packed with helpful information, including wire sizing, switch-installation schematics, cable-routing details, appliance wattage, doorbell hook-ups, typical service panel circuitry and much more. A glossary of terms is also included.

CONSTRUCTION

The Blueprint Package contains information an experienced builder needs to construct a particular house. However, it doesn't show all the ways that houses can be built, nor does it explain alternate construction methods. To help you understand how your house will be built—and offer additional techniques—this set of Construction Details depicts the materials and methods used to build foundations, fireplaces, walls, floors and roofs. Where appropriate, the drawings show acceptable alternatives.

MECHANICAL

These Mechanical Details contain fundamental principles and useful data that will help you make informed decisions and communicate with subcontractors about heating and cooling systems. Drawings contain instructions and samples that allow you to make simple load calculations, and preliminary sizing and costing analysis. Covered are the most commonly used systems from heat pumps to solar fuel systems. The package is filled with illustrations and diagrams to help you visualize components and how they relate to one another.

THE HANDS-ON HOME FURNITURE PLANNER

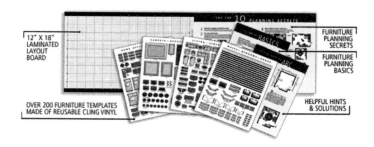

Effectively plan the space in your home using The **Hands-On Home Furniture Planner**. It's fun and easy—no more moving heavy pieces of furniture to see how the room will go together. And you can try different layouts, moving furniture at a whim.

The kit includes reusable peel and stick furniture templates that fit onto a 12" x 18" laminated layout board—space enough to layout every room in your home.

Also included in the package are a number of helpful planning tools. You'll receive:

✓ Helpful hints and solutions for difficult situations.
✓ Furniture planning basics to get you started.
✓ Furniture planning secrets that let you in on some of the tricks of professional designers.

The **Hands-On Home Furniture Planner** is the one tool that no new homeowner or home remodeler should be without. It's also a perfect housewarming gift!

To Order, Call Toll Free
1-800-521-6797

After you've looked over our Blueprint Package and Important Extras on these pages, call for current pricing and availability prior to mailing the order form. We're ready and eager to serve you. After you have received your order, call for customer service toll free 1-888-690-1116.

HOUSE BLUEPRINT PRICE SCHEDULE

Prices guaranteed through December 31, 2003

TIERS	1-SET STUDY PACKAGE	4-SET BUILDING PACKAGE	8-SET BUILDING PACKAGE	1-SET REPRODUCIBLE*
A1	$440	$480	$520	$660
A2	$480	$520	$560	$720
A3	$530	$575	$615	$800
A4	$575	$620	$660	$870
C1	$620	$665	$710	$935
C2	$670	$715	$760	$1000
C3	$715	$760	$805	$1075
C4	$765	$810	$855	$1150
L1	$870	$925	$975	$1300
L2	$945	$1000	$1050	$1420
L3	$1050	$1105	$1155	$1575
L4	$1155	$1210	$1260	$1735

* Requires a fax number

TO USE THE INDEX:

Refer to the design number listed in numerical order (a helpful page reference is also given). Note the price tier and refer to the House Blueprint Price Schedule above for the cost of one, four or eight sets of blueprints or the cost of a reproducible drawing. Additional prices are shown for identical and reverse blueprint sets, as well as a very useful Materials List for some of the plans. The letter "Y" identifies plans that are part of our Quote One® estimating service and those that offer Materials Lists.

TO ORDER, Call toll free 1-800-521-6797 for current pricing and availability prior to mailing the order form. FAX: 1-800-224-6699 or 520-544-3086.

OPTIONS FOR PLANS IN TIERS A1–L4

Additional Identical Blueprints
in same order for "A1-L4" price plans ....$50 per set
Reverse Blueprints (mirror image)
with 4- or 8-set order for "A1–L4" plans..........................$50 fee per order
Specification Outlines..$10 each
Materials Lists for "A1–C3" plans ....$60 each
Materials Lists for "C4–L4" plans..$70 each

IMPORTANT NOTES

• The 1-set study package is marked "not for construction."
• Prices for 4- or 8-set Building Packages honored only at time of original order.
• Some foundations carry a $225 surcharge.
• Right-reading reverse blueprints, if available, will incur a $165 surcharge.
• Additional identical blueprints may be purchased within 60 days of original order.

PLAN INDEX

DESIGN	PRICE	PAGE	MATERIALS LIST	QUOTE ONE®
HPT260001	L3	4		
HPT260002	L3	5		
HPT260003	L3	6		
HPT260004	A4	7		
HPT260005	C2	8		
HPT260006	C2	9		
HPT260007	C1	10		
HPT260008	C1	11		
HPT260009	C1	12		
HPT260010	C1	13		
HPT260011	L2	14		
HPT260012	L3	15		

BEFORE FILLING OUT

THE ORDER FORM,

PLEASE CALL US ON

OUR TOLL-FREE

BLUEPRINT HOTLINE

1-800-521-6797.

YOU MAY WANT TO

LEARN MORE ABOUT

OUR SERVICES AND

PRODUCTS. HERE'S

SOME INFORMATION

YOU WILL FIND HELPFUL.

OUR EXCHANGE POLICY

With the exception of reproducible plan orders, we will exchange your entire first order for an equal or greater number of blueprints within our plan collection within 90 days of the original order. The entire content of your original order must be returned before an exchange will be processed. Please call our customer service department for your return authorization number and shipping instructions. If the returned blueprints look used, redlined or copied, we will not honor your exchange. Fees for exchanging your blueprints are as follows: 20% of the amount of the original order...plus the difference in cost if exchanging for a design in a higher price bracket or less the difference in cost if exchanging for a design in a lower price bracket. **(Reproducible blueprints are not exchangeable or refundable.)** Please call for current postage and handling prices. Shipping and handling charges are not refundable.

ABOUT REPRODUCIBLES

When purchasing a reproducible you may be required to furnish a fax number. The designer will fax documents that you must sign and return to them before shipping will take place.

ABOUT REVERSE BLUEPRINTS

Although lettering and dimensions will appear backward, reverses will be a useful aid if you decide to flop the plan. See Price Schedule and Plans Index for pricing.

REVISING, MODIFYING AND CUSTOMIZING PLANS

Like many homeowners who buy these plans, you and your builder, architect or engineer may want to make changes to them. We recommend purchase of a reproducible plan for any changes made by your builder, licensed architect or engineer. As set forth below, we cannot assume any responsibility for blueprints which have been changed, whether by you, your builder or by professionals selected by you or referred to you by us, because such individuals are outside our supervision and control.

ARCHITECTURAL AND ENGINEERING SEALS

Some cities and states are now requiring that a licensed architect or engineer review and "seal" a blueprint, or officially approve it, prior to construction due to concerns over energy costs, safety and other factors. Prior to application for a building permit or the start of actual construction, we strongly advise that you consult your local building official who can tell you if such a review is required.

ABOUT THE DESIGNS

The architects and designers whose work appears in this publication are among America's leading residential designers. Each plan was designed to meet the requirements of a nationally recognized model building code in effect at the time and place the plan was drawn. Because national building codes change from time to time, plans may not comply with any such code at the time they are sold to a customer. In addition, building officials may not accept these plans as final construction documents of record as the plans may need to be modified and additional drawings and details added to suit local conditions and requirements. We strongly advise that purchasers consult a licensed architect or engineer, and their local building official, before starting any construction related to these plans.

LOCAL BUILDING CODES AND ZONING REQUIREMENTS

At the time of creation, our plans are drawn to specifications published by the Building Officials and Code Administrators (BOCA) International, Inc.; the Southern Building Code Congress (SBCCI) International, Inc.; the International Conference of Building Officials (ICBO); or the Council of American Building Officials (CABO). Our plans are designed to meet or exceed national building standards. Because of the great differences in geography and climate throughout the United States and Canada, each state, county and municipality has its own building codes, zone requirements, ordinances and building regulations. Your plan may need to be modified to comply with local requirements regarding snow loads, energy codes, soil and seismic conditions and a wide range of other matters. In addition, you may need to obtain permits or inspections from local governments before and in the course of construction. Prior to using blueprints ordered from us, we strongly advise that you consult a licensed architect or engineer—and speak with your local building official—before applying for any permit or beginning construction. We authorize the use of our blueprints on the express condition that you strictly comply with all local building codes, zoning requirements and other applicable laws, regulations, ordinances and requirements. Notice: Plans for homes to be built in Nevada must be re-drawn by a Nevada-registered professional. Consult your building official for more information on this subject.

TOLL FREE
1-800-521-6797

REGULAR OFFICE HOURS:
8:00 a.m.-9:00 p.m. EST, Monday-Friday

If we receive your order by 3:00 p.m. EST, Monday-Friday, we'll process it and ship within **two business days**. When ordering by phone, please have your credit card or check information ready. We'll also ask you for the Order Form Key Number at the bottom of the order form.

By FAX: Copy the Order Form on the next page and send it on our FAX line: 1-800-224-6699 or 520-544-3086.

Canadian Customers
Order Toll Free 1-877-223-6389

ORDER FORM

CALL FOR CURRENT PRICING & AVAILABILITY
PRIOR TO MAILING THIS ORDER FORM.

DISCLAIMER

The designers we work with have put substantial care and effort into the creation of their blueprints. However, because they cannot provide on-site consultation, supervision and control over actual construction, and because of the great variance in local building requirements, building practices and soil, seismic, weather and other conditions, WE CANNOT MAKE ANY WARRANTY, EXPRESS OR IMPLIED, WITH RESPECT TO THE CONTENT OR USE OF THE BLUEPRINTS, INCLUDING BUT NOT LIMITED TO ANY WARRANTY OF MERCHANTABILITY OR OF FITNESS FOR A PARTICULAR PURPOSE. ITEMS, PRICES, TERMS AND CONDITIONS ARE SUBJECT TO CHANGE WITHOUT NOTICE. REPRODUCIBLE PLAN ORDERS MAY REQUIRE A CUSTOMER'S SIGNED RELEASE BEFORE SHIPPING.

TERMS AND CONDITIONS

These designs are protected under the terms of United States Copyright Law and may not be copied or reproduced in any way, by any means, unless you have purchased Reproducibles which clearly indicate your right to copy or reproduce. We authorize the use of your chosen design as an aid in the construction of one single family home only. You may not use this design to build a second or multiple dwellings without purchasing another blueprint or blueprints or paying additional design fees.

HOW MANY BLUEPRINTS DO YOU NEED?

Although a standard building package may satisfy many states, cities and counties, some plans may require certain changes. For your convenience, we have developed a Reproducible plan which allows a local professional to modify and make up to 10 copies of your revised plan. As our plans are all copyright protected, with your purchase of the Reproducible, we will supply you with a Copyright release letter. The number of copies you may need: 1 for owner; 3 for builder; 2 for local building department and 1-3 sets for your mortgage lender.

☎ ORDER TOLL FREE!

**For information about
any of our services
or to order call
1-800-521-6797**

**Browse our website:
www.eplans.com**

**BLUEPRINTS ARE
NOT REFUNDABLE
EXCHANGES ONLY**

**For Customer Service,
call toll free
1-888-690-1116.**

HOME PLANNERS, LLC wholly owned by Hanley-Wood, LLC
3275 WEST INA ROAD, SUITE 110 • TUCSON, ARIZONA • 85741

THE BASIC BLUEPRINT PACKAGE

Rush me the following (please refer to the Plans Index and Price Schedule in this section):

___Set(s) of reproducibles*, plan number(s) _____ $_____
    indicate foundation type _____ surcharge (if applicable): $_____
___Set(s) of blueprints, plan number(s) _____ indicate foundation type _____
    indicate foundation type _____ surcharge (if applicable): $_____
___Additional identical blueprints (standard or reverse) in same order @ $50 per set $_____
___Reverse blueprints @ $50 fee per order. Right-reading reverse @ $165 surcharge $_____

IMPORTANT EXTRAS

Rush me the following:

___Materials List: $60 (Must be purchased with Blueprint set.) Add $10 for Schedule C4–L4 plans $_____
___**Quote One**® Summary Cost Report @ $29.95 for one, $14.95 for each additional,
    for plans _____ $_____
    Building location: City _____ Zip Code _____
___**Quote One**® Material Cost Report @ $120 Schedules P1–C3; $130 Schedules C4–L4,
    for plan_____(Must be purchased with Blueprints set.) $_____
    Building location: City _____ Zip Code _____
___Specification Outlines @ $10 each $_____
___Detail Sets @ $14.95 each; any two $22.95; any three $29.95; all four for $39.95 (save $19.85) $_____
    ❑ Plumbing ❑ Electrical ❑ Construction ❑ Mechanical
___Home Furniture Planner @ $15.95 each $_____

DECK BLUEPRINTS

(Please refer to the Plans Index and Price Schedule in this section)

___Set(s) of Deck Plan _____. $_____
___Additional identical blueprints in same order @ $10 per set. $_____
___Reverse blueprints @ $10 fee per order. $_____
___Set of Standard Deck Details @ $14.95 per set. $_____
___Set of Complete Deck Construction Package (Best Buy!) Add $10 to Building Package.
    Includes Custom Deck Plan _____ Plus Standard Deck Details

LANDSCAPE BLUEPRINTS

(Please refer to the Plans Index and Price Schedule in this section.)

___Set(s) of Landscape Plan _____ $_____
___Additional identical blueprints in same order @ $10 per set $_____
___Reverse blueprints @ $10 fee per order $_____

Please indicate appropriate region of the country for Plant & Material List. Region _____

POSTAGE AND HANDLING *SIGNATURE IS REQUIRED FOR ALL DELIVERIES.*	1–3 sets	4+ sets
DELIVERY		
No CODs (Requires street address—No P.O. Boxes)		
•Regular Service (Allow 7–10 business days delivery)	❑ $20.00	❑ $25.00
•Priority (Allow 4–5 business days delivery)	❑ $25.00	❑ $35.00
•Express (Allow 3 business days delivery)	❑ $35.00	❑ $45.00
OVERSEAS DELIVERY	fax, phone or mail for quote	

Note: All delivery times are from date Blueprint Package is shipped.

POSTAGE (From box above) $_____
SUBTOTAL $_____
SALES TAX (AZ & MI residents, please add appropriate state and local sales tax.) $_____
TOTAL (Subtotal and tax) $_____

YOUR ADDRESS (please print legibly)

Name _____

Street_____

City _____ State_____ Zip _____

Daytime telephone number (required) (_____) _____

* Fax number (required for reproducible orders) _____
TeleCheck® Checks By Phone℠ available

FOR CREDIT CARD ORDERS ONLY

Credit card number _____ Exp. Date: (M/Y) _____

Check one ❑ Visa ❑ MasterCard ❑ Discover Card ❑ American Express

Order Form Key

HPT262

Signature (required) _____

Please check appropriate box: ❑ Licensed Builder-Contractor ❑ Homeowner

---

 ORDER TOLL FREE!
1-800-521-6797

BY FAX: Copy the order form above and send it on our FAXLINE: 1-800-224-6699 OR 520-544-3086

1 BIGGEST & BEST

1001 of our best-selling plans in one volume. 1,074 to 7,275 square feet. 704 pgs $12.95 1K1

2 ONE-STORY

450 designs for all lifestyles. 800 to 4,900 square feet. 384 pgs $9.95 OS

3 MORE ONE-STORY

475 superb one-level plans from 800 to 5,000 square feet. 448 pgs $9.95 MO2

4 TWO-STORY

443 designs for one-and-a-half and two stories. 1,500 to 6,000 square feet. 448 pgs $9.95 TS

5 VACATION

430 designs for recreation, retirement and leisure. 448 pgs $9.95 VS3

6 HILLSIDE

208 designs for split-levels, bi-levels, multi-levels and walkouts. 224 pgs $9.95 HH

7 FARMHOUSE

300 Fresh Designs from Classic to Modern. 320 pgs. $10.95 FCP

8 COUNTRY HOUSES

208 unique home plans that combine traditional style and modern livability. 224 pgs $9.95 CN

9 BUDGET-SMART

200 efficient plans from 7 top designers, that you can really afford to build! 224 pgs $8.95 BS

10 BARRIER-FREE

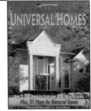

Over 1,700 products and 51 plans for accessible living. 128 pgs $15.95 UH

11 ENCYCLOPEDIA

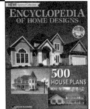

500 exceptional plans for all styles and budgets—the best book of its kind! 528 pgs $9.95 ENC

12 ENCYCLOPEDIA II

500 completely new plans. Spacious and stylish designs for every budget and taste. 352 pgs $9.95 E2

13 AFFORDABLE

300 Modest plans for savvy homebuyers. 256 pgs. $9.95 AH2

14 VICTORIAN

210 striking Victorian and Farmhouse designs from today's top designers. 224 pgs $15.95 VDH2

15 ESTATE

Dream big! Eighteen designers showcase their biggest and best plans. 224 pgs $16.95 EDH3

16 LUXURY

170 lavish designs, over 50% brand-new plans added to a most elegant collection. 192 pgs $12.95 LD3

17 EUROPEAN STYLES

200 homes with a unique flair of the Old World. 224 pgs $15.95 EURO

18 COUNTRY CLASSICS

Donald Gardner's 101 best Country and Traditional home plans. 192 pgs $17.95 DAG

19 COUNTRY

85 Charming Designs from American Home Gallery. 160 pgs. $17.95 CTY

20 TRADITIONAL

85 timeless designs from the Design Traditions Library. 160 pgs $17.95 TRA

21 COTTAGES

245 Delightful retreats from 825 to 3,500 square feet. 256 pgs. $10.95 COOL

22 CABINS TO VILLAS

Enchanting Homes for Mountain Sea or Sun, from the Sater collection. 144 pgs $19.95 CCV

23 CONTEMPORARY

The most complete and imaginative collection of contemporary designs available anywhere. 256 pgs. $10.95 CM2

24 FRENCH COUNTRY

Live every day in the French countryside using these plans, landscapes and interiors. 192 pgs. $14.95 PN

25 SOUTHERN

207 homes rich in Southern styling and comfort. 240 pgs $8.95 SH

26 SOUTHWESTERN

138 designs that capture the spirit of the Southwest. 144 pgs $10.95 SW

27 SHINGLE-STYLE

155 Home plans from Classic Colonials to Breezy Bungalows. 192 pgs. $12.95 SNG

28 NEIGHBORHOOD

170 designs with the feel of main street America. 192 pgs $12.95 TND

29 CRAFTSMAN

170 Home plans in the Craftsman and Bungalow style. 192 pgs $12.95 CC

30 GRAND VISTAS

200 Homes with a View. 224 pgs. $10.95 GV

31 DUPLEX & TOWNHOMES

115 Duplex, Multiplex & Townhome Designs. 128 pgs. $17.95 MFH

32 WATERFRONT

200 designs perfect for your waterside wonderland. 208 pgs $10.95 WF

33 NATURAL LIGHT

223 Sunny home plans for all regions. 240 pgs. $8.95 NA

34 NOSTALGIA

100 Time-Honored designs updated with today's features. 224 pgs. $14.95 NOS

35 STREET OF DREAMS

Over 300 photos showcase 54 prestigious homes. 256 pgs $19.95 SOD

36 NARROW-LOT

250 Designs for houses 17' to 50' wide. 256 pgs. $9.95 NL2

37 SMALL HOUSES

Innovative plans for sensible lifestyles. 224 pgs. $8.95 SM2

38 GARDENS & MORE

225 gardens, landscapes, decks and more to enhance every home. 320 pgs. $19.95 GLP

39 EASY-CARE

41 special landscapes designed for beauty and low maintenance. 160 pgs $14.95 ECL

40 BACKYARDS

40 designs focused solely on creating your own specially themed backyard oasis. 160 pgs $14.95 BYL

41 BEDS & BORDERS

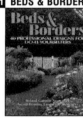

40 Professional designs for do-it-yourselfers. 160 pgs. $14.95 BB

42 BUYER'S GUIDE

A comprehensive look at 2700 products for all aspects of landscaping & gardening. 128 pgs $19.95 LPBG

LANDSCAPE DESIGNS

43 OUTDOOR

74 easy-to-build designs, lets you create and build your own backyard oasis. 128 pgs $9.95 YG2

44 GARAGES

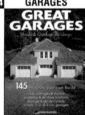

145 exciting projects from 64 to 1,900 square feet. 160 pgs. $9.95 GG2

45 DECKS

A brand new collection of 120 beautiful and practical decks. 144 pgs. $9.95 DP2

46 HOME BUILDING

Everything you need to know to work with contractors and subcontractors. 212 pgs $14.95 HBP

47 RURAL BUILDING

Everything you need to know to build your home in the country. 232 pgs. $14.95 BYC

48 VACATION HOMES

Your complete guide to building your vacation home. 224 pgs. $14.95 BYV

PROJECT GUIDES

Book Order Form

To order your books, just check the box of the book numbered below and complete the coupon. We will process your order and ship it from our office within two business days. Send coupon and check (in U.S. funds).

YES! Please send me the books I've indicated:

- 1:1K1 ....$12.95
- 2:OS $9.95
- 3:MO2.........$9.95
- 4:TS $9.95
- 5:VS3 ....$9.95
- 6:HH............$9.95
- 7:FCP $10.95
- 8:CN $9.95
- 9:BS $8.95
- 10:UH $15.95
- 11:ENC.........$9.95
- 12:E2 ....$9.95
- 13:AH2........$9.95
- 14:VDH2....$15.95
- 15:EDH3....$16.95
- 16:LD3......$12.95

- 17:EURO...$15.95
- 18:DAG $17.95
- 19:CTY......$17.95
- 20:TRA......$17.95
- 21:COOL...$10.95
- 22:CCV......$19.95
- 23:CM2......$10.95
- 24:PN $14.95
- 25:SH $8.95
- 26:SW.......$10.95
- 27:SNG $12.95
- 28:TND $12.95
- 29:CC $12.95
- 30:GV........$10.95
- 31:MFH....$17.95
- 32:WF $10.95

- 33:NA..........$8.95
- 34:NOS $14.95
- 35:SOD $19.95
- 36:NL2........$9.95
- 37:SM2........$8.95
- 38:GLP......$19.95
- 39:ECL......$14.95
- 40:BYL......$14.95
- 41:BB $14.95
- 42:LPBG $19.95
- 43:YG2........$9.95
- 44:GG2 ....$9.95
- 45:DP2........$9.95
- 46:HBP $14.95
- 47:BYC......$14.95
- 48:BYV......$14.95

Books Subtotal $_____
ADD Postage and Handling (allow 4–6 weeks for delivery) $ 4.00
Sales Tax: (AZ & MI residents, add state and local sales tax.) $_____
YOUR TOTAL (Subtotal, Postage/Handling, Tax) $_____

YOUR ADDRESS (PLEASE PRINT)

Name _____
Street _____
City _____State _____Zip _____
Phone (_____) _____—_____

YOUR PAYMENT

TeleCheck® Checks By Phone℠ available
Check one: ❏ Check ❏ Visa ❏ MasterCard ❏ Discover ❏ American Express
Required credit card information:

Credit Card Number _____
Expiration Date (Month/Year)_____/ _____
Signature Required _____

Home Planners, LLC
3275 W. Ina Road, Suite 110, Dept. BK, Tucson, AZ 85741

HPT262

Canadian Customers Order Toll Free 1-877-223-6389

FOR FASTER SERVICE ORDER ONLINE AT
www.hwspecials.com

HEAT-N-GLO
1-888-427-3973
WWW.HEATNGLO.COM

Heat-N-Glo offers quality gas, woodburning and electric fireplaces, including gas log sets, stoves, and inserts for preexisting fireplaces. Now available gas grills and outdoor fireplaces. Send for a free brochure.

Ideas for your next project. Beautiful, durable, elegant low-maintenance millwork, mouldings, balustrade systems and much more. For your free catalog please call us at 1-800-446-3040 or visit www.stylesolutionsinc.com.

ARISTOKRAFT
ONE MASTERBRAND CABINETS DRIVE
JASPER, IN 47546
(812) 482-2527
WWW.ARISTOKRAFT.COM

Aristokraft offers you superb value, outstanding quality and great style that fit your budget. Transform your great ideas into reality with popular styles and features that reflect your taste and lifestyle. $5.00

THERMA-TRU DOORS
1687 WOODLANDS DRIVE
MAUMEE, OH 43537
1-800-THERMA-TRU
WWW.THERMATRU.COM

The undisputed brand leader, Therma-Tru specializes in fiberglass and steel entry doors for every budget. Excellent craftsmanship, energy efficiency and variety make Therma-Tru the perfect choice for all your entry door needs.

---

225 GARDEN, LANDSCAPE
AND PROJECT PLANS
TO ORDER, CALL
1-800-322-6797

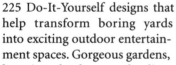

225 Do-It-Yourself designs that help transform boring yards into exciting outdoor entertainment spaces. Gorgeous gardens, luxurious landscapes, dazzling decks and other outdoor amenities. Complete construction blueprints available for every project. Only $19.95 (plus $4 shipping/handling).

HAVE WE GOT PLANS FOR YOU!

Your online source for home designs and ideas. Find thousands of plans from the nation's top designers...all in one place. Plus, links to the best known names in building supplies and services.